Harry Drabik's Guide to Wilderness Canoeing

Illustrated by Randall W. Scholes

Nodin Press
Minneapolis, Minnesota

ISBN-0-931714-31-1

Nodin Press, a division of Micawber's, Inc.
525 North Third Street,
Minneapolis, MN 55401

Dedicated To Two Guides

Brian Hoffman and Jesse Pash.
Two who learned their craft well.
Two who were faithful.
Two who made me happy
to have travelled with them.

Harry Drabik lives in a refurbished log cabin on the north shore of Lake Superior near the Boundary Waters Canoe Area Wilderness. In recent years he has turned his energies toward heritage resources and the study of prehistory, having been for years an archaeologist in the Province of Ontario. He is also the author of THE SPIRIT OF CANOE CAMPING and THE SPIRIT OF WINTER CAMPING. He is currently at work on a book of wilderness essays.

Table of Contents

I

The Skills and
Topics of a Guide

Guiding—You Do *What* for a Living?

For years I've heard it from my friends and relatives in Chicago. They wonder how I can "survive." They show amazement that I was able to "pry" myself away from the North to visit them. And every one of them has asked some version of the question: What do you do with yourself all winter when everything's frozen solid?

I hear it from strangers, too. Recently, I was introduced to a professional woman in the Twin Cities. When our host identified me as a Canoe Country guide, the woman looked puzzled, slightly startled, and said, "Well, you're certainly out of your element down here. If I were able to live up North, I'd *never* come back."

Such reactions highlight common perceptions about guiding. A guide is out of place outside wilderness. A guide is unusual, out-of-the-ordinary. Some attach reverence toward a worker who conducts his affairs in nature's cathedral. And quite often, people see guiding as a reclusive occupation not relating to people or to *normal* human activity. For many, guiding is a romantic throwback, loaded with trite movie images, and having no useful, earthly application. A guide is seen as an oddity. He's a quaint "character" onto which one can graft an escapist fantasy or two, but beyond that, having no utility.

I want to say at the start that the contents of this book are not dedicated to perpetuating a vanishing way of life nor toward encouraging idle daydreams—a guide's work is too pragmatic for that. My aim, instead, is to provide insights into living with, working with, and instructing people; a process that is the same in city or country. When not doing that, I will try to provide practical pointers about campcraft or equipment.

On the pages that follow, you'll find a mixture of information that relates, as much as possible, to day-to-day concerns. In fact, you are apt to find a few things that will describe something in your living or working situation. I won't be surprised if you do, because *you* may be a guide, too.

You see, while we associate the word "guide" with the outdoors and an exotic way of life, guides are, in actuality, quite common, most being found in urban settings. Guiding behavior is human behavior, found at many levels of personal and social activity.

For example, when I travel outside Canoe Country I am no longer guiding. Instead, others guide me, first to the correct boarding area for my flight. Next, a pilot and crew act on my behalf, just as I do for clients on a canoe trip. When we land, ground-crew people will guide my luggage along, and then a taxi driver will be my next guide over the unfamiliar territory of a city I've not visited before. Following that, my hotel clerk, telephone operators, receptionists, etc. will all provide information and help me with appointments and directions. Guiding is very much a part of many occupations that are taken for granted as part of everyday life in civilization.

These jobs may lack the trappings and romance of wilderness, but the behavior pattern involved is that of a guide.

And of course I've yet to mention the obvious guiding jobs of parents, clergy, counselors, physicians, and teachers. Rather than feeling alone with an unusual occupation, I feel quite at home—part of a large fraternity of service.

It is curious, though, that when guiding is mentioned, people think of the outdoor guide, perhaps because the wilderness guide is the elite of the fraternity. Not in terms of income, mind you, but in most big companies the more important executives get the bigger offices. My office and workspace is over one million acres, and the photo murals on my walls are the real thing.

Seriously though, guiding isn't an adventure into obscura. It is part of us as a people, and it includes skills that all of us want.

The Sought-For Skills

Honesty. No, I'm not going to moralize or preach, because my appreciation of honesty is practical, not philosophical. Let me tell a story. Before one of my trips, a food order hadn't arrived and I had to improvise an evening meal from items on hand. I threw together ingredients and called the result "Ham 'n Bean Surprise." It was tempting to try to pass the "Surprise" off as a regular meal, thus saving myself the bother of having to explain what happened to the correct meal. But I didn't. Instead, I told my clients I was sorry, and that one of the meals I'd ordered hadn't been shipped and I had to invent something to take its place. And that's how I introduced "Ham 'n Bean Surprise," which turned out like seasoned sawdust with pink chunks in it. We all had a good laugh about the blandest, ugliest meal that ever went down—or, rather, didn't.

My clients hadn't been lied to and they proved capable of living with a less than perfect item on the menu. On my side, I didn't have to try to remember a "story" or defend a substandard meal by claiming it usually turned out good. I'm sure, too, that even a well-told lie would still sound hollow, tainting a guide's work. When we returned from our trip the missing case was waiting, along with a note of apology from the shipper.

Patience. Because I know my craft, it's sometimes difficult for me to keep my cool while clients halt and stumble along on a simple task. I get tired of having to remind people (over and over) of the correct way to load a canoe, come into a landing, pack a packsack, carry the food pack, and help with cleanup. On most trips I can look forward to at least three days of constantly having to repeat simple instructions. It's enough to make me lose my patience.

But all I have to do is put myself in their position. If outdoor camping were new to me, it would take a few days before I was able to perform the required tasks easily. When I'm visiting an urban area, I know it takes me several times over an auto route before I know the way, and I have to stay constantly alert and work at it, too. Yet the same route is second nature to my clients. Knowing what I'm like outside my element goes a long way toward providing the patience I need to work with people outside of theirs.

I've had to work on patience more than any other skill, and it got more important as I got to be a more proficient guide/instructor. You see, as your presentation improves there's a tendency to expect people to do better. After all, you're doing your best and keeping it as simple as possible — why, anyone *should* be able to catch on. But it's not that the clients are stupid or that the instruction isn't clear. It simply takes time for instruction to sort itself out into behavior, and that calls for patience on the part of the guide, especially if he or she is proficient and eager to do a good job.

Understanding. Now there's one of those magic words that's so often talked about. In one respect it means sympathy, which won't count for much in the bush. In another respect it means experience, which will count in the bush.

Let me explain with an example. I understand people (in some situations) because I've experience working with them. Without ample past experience, understanding is limited. I *know* that each time I ask new clients if they've paddled before, they will nearly all nod and indicate they're experienced, capable, ready-to-go. In reality they have done little paddling and have probably received minimal instruction in the past. Because of my "understanding," I know that not one of them will confess to being ignorant. After all, who wants to look foolish or appear to be a tenderfoot by making a public confession?

Understanding also gives me the clue needed to instruct them without their having to admit to being greenhorns. After they affirm by word or gesture, that they are experienced I say, "Good. That will make it easier for all of us. But, just to brush up, let me show you the basic strokes. That way we'll share the same terminology, and it will be less confusing." They then do *me* the favor of watching my instruction and spending time on practice, which is exactly what I was after. The use of understanding can lead to quite pragmatic results.

Tact. One of the hardest parts of guiding is to correct a person and not have it become a put-down. Especially the first day or two, before I know my clients and they've had a chance to adjust to me, being tactful about suggestions and procedures is vitally important. It is so crucial I've had to give myself a general principle to follow and adhere to strictly: "Correct a behavior or procedure — never correct a person."

Commenting on a behavior is neutral territory as far as correction goes. Done objectively and in a helpful manner, correction is not an affront to personal dignity. My approach runs like this: "Here, let me give you a hand, and I'll show you a way to make it easier" or "You're doing fine, but next time try doing those one at a time, instead of together." Such instruction is intended to be practical and make things easier.

Woe unto the guide who says, "That's a *dumb* way to do it. Here, I'll show you the *right* way." Such an approach inflates the guide's ego at the expense of client dignity. More unfortunate than that, it creates an emotionally loaded situation, which is hard to work in and not nearly as relaxed and friendly as it could be if tact were used.

Approachability. A highly skilled expert with unqualified credentials may know more about the outdoors, nature, wildlife, and camping than any other human alive, but for all that he won't make a good guide if his personality sets him above his clients. Guiding is not a matter of sending orders and direction down from on high. It is a matter of working through procedure, technique, and information with people engaged in a combined effort.

From my experience, approachability has two components. These are: Friendliness and Good Humor. An honestly friendly person is attractive to others. So a guide should be friendly because it is a genuine part of him. Guiding isn't a job for hermits, snobs, or complainers. You've got to like people, like working with them, and like being of service. Couple that with good humor and you've got an approachable guide who is more coach than dictator.

And believe me, good humor is important. I make it a point to tell a joke on myself or point out my own foibles early in a trip. That way, clients can see that I won't approach mistakes harshly. Innocent, happy humor sets a tone for the days to follow, and, let's face it, life being what it is, there will be days in the bush when a person will need all the good humor he or she can muster. Even serious matters often need to be tempered with a smile and nod of friendly assurance. While for many, angry muttering is standard fare, a thoughtful guide will know the twinkle in his eye is the reflection of the warmth of his spirit, and he will always prefer to use attraction and joint concern as opposed to sullen order giving.

Clarity. A well-trained, fully prepared guide with an appealing persona may still flop if he lacks clarity. If clients feel unsure of what's going on, of who is in charge, of what the rules are, of how to do tasks, then the guide has probably been unclear in giving direction, or has failed to do so entirely,

14

as an oversight. I have seen guides so fearful of making a mistake that they exercise no leadership. In other cases the guide assumes that giving instructions *once* will suffice, or he assumes clients to be as familiar as he with camping skills. I once watched a frustrated young guide grow more and more perturbed as he shouted instructions to a novice who floated thirty feet away. I could see the novice growing uneasy and more confused as the guide shouted and gestured, in what looked more like a display of anger than instruction. The guide could not instruct nor could the beginner learn—not with thirty feet between them.

In many cases when instruction fails, it fails from a lack of clarity. The teaching situation needs to be one where people can see and hear well. If practice is needed, it should be conducted under a condition that allows for monitoring and close-at-hand correction. A guide must repeat important instructions, explain as needed, define terms, and seek to be questioned. All of this is done to facilitate the learning process, with the immediate, functional goal of creating a smoother camping experience for all. I've heard guides complain about their "dumb" clients, but when clients fail to perform well it is as much a fault of guide instruction as it is of client learning.

I always try to break tasks into segments, thus generating a series of small learning steps rather than one, big lesson. I repeat things often and attempt to organize the more difficult tasks, like portaging, by utilizing client comments. By actively assuming my share of the responsibility for client learning, I usually catch problems or misunderstandings early, thus getting them out of the way. And, of course, all this instructing and organizing is done in an open, friendly way.

Quite often someone on a trip will question me about why I do something a particular way. Being helpful, they will usually explain to me a "better" way. My task, however, is to keep instruction from becoming loaded or emotional, which comments about a "right way" versus a "wrong way" are apt to do. I handle comments about "better" ways to do thing with the following tactic—I always acknowledge, with thanks, the helpful suggestion and I always say the suggestion as well as the procedure I follow are both "good." For many tasks there are a number of workable ways, and I do not quibble about which is "best." In essence, that sort of position on my part is a matter of politeness, but it must be clear and honest in order to work. I'm also being clear when I sometimes explain, "I do it this way because I prefer it." The statement reflects bias, but it is clear, and people do accept personal (or organizational) preference as a valid reason. For harmony on a trip, it's wise never to defend a personal bias by claiming it's the "better" way.

Thoroughness. Early in my guiding career I had a party arrive hours late, which meant that organizing our departure for the same day was more hectic than usual. I felt rather proud of myself for being able to start from behind and still have a successful first day, which got us a short but reasonable distance into the wilderness. That evening, my assistant and a few others went fishing and returned with two very nice smallmouth bass and a smallish walleye. Once filleted, the fish made a splendid addition to the next morning's breakfast.

Sounds good, doesn't it? Fresh fried fish to go along with scrambled eggs — a truly excellent wilderness repast. That's what I thought, too. In fact, the entire group was eagerly awaiting their taste of fresh fish. They eyed the fillets, they helped soap the griddle, they made sure we had a perfect fire, but we were missing one little thing. There was no oil for frying. Where was it? It was with the margarine in a plastic container back home in my refrigerator. In the confusion of the previous day I'd left it there, intending to retrieve it later, and I'd simply forgotten it.

It was a small mistake, but what a sad one! And unfortunately, oil for frying is not something a person can improvise in the bush. That occurence taught me that memory alone will not suffice when one has to cope with meeting new people and unforseen events. No matter how often I'd been into the bush, I could still forget things if I didn't write them down. That's how I started to make and use checklists. Before leaving, I now go over every item on the list at least *twice*. The cooking oil no longer gets left behind.

Beyond being careful enough to ensure that all needed equipment and supplies are present, one must be thorough and exact in the execution of camping details. For example, each of my tents has a number on it. That way it's easy for people to get the same tent each time we make camp, and if something's missing or "wrong," well, they can't blame it on someone else's negligence. It's the same for many camping details. If I want people to retrieve *all* of their tent stakes, I have to help them to do so. On each tent stake sack, therefore, I've boldly written the number of stakes that go inside. The number serves to remind them to double check, which is much easier than having to improvise pegs after you've lost them.

All my sleeping bags are numbered, because with identical bags there is hardly another way for people to be sure of getting the same bag each night. My life jackets have a size and number printed on them, and I go so far as to *assign* a properly fitting jacket to each person. No guesswork there. A strict, thorough procedure assures that each paddler has an appropriate safety device, because it's no good if it doesn't fit right. Around the cooking area we institute a rule to keep people from underfoot while the cooks work. And the cooks are often reminded *never* to set a pot of food on a log or stump. Why? Because when you place a pot on firm, level ground it can't fall and spill. A pot perched on a log invites disaster.

Detail upon detail goes into making a trip smooth, efficient, and enjoyable. It is, after all, no fun to have people grumping at one another because they are hungry (the pot of stew slipped off a log, so they didn't get much to eat). Thorough attention to detail is the most human way I know of to make a wilderness trip a pleasant adventure as opposed to a frustrating series of mishaps.

The Sought-For Craft

The ability of a guide to function in the bush is often envied and admired. As with any craft, one gets better with experience or practice, and the learning process continues, even after many years of doing the activity.

You may wonder why I put craft at the end of my list of guide qualifications. I'm quite aware that I talked much more about personality traits than campcraft tests. It's my opinion that personality counts for a great deal in guiding. As far as I'm concerned, the really important characteristics of guiding are intimately useful in parenting, professional work, or conducting one's self in a vocational trade.

I also downplay craft because a good guide tries to keep skills on a simple, functional level. Ninety-nine percent of any trip is comprised of routine details that consist of camping basics. One packs, paddles, unpacks, sets up a tent, airs a sleeping bag, cooks, etc. — all of which are basic acts that can be accomplished by novices. Only rarely does a trip slip over the brink and call for anything clever or advanced. On occasion, a personal emergency or injury may require unusual effort. Almost never will one have to fend off marauding wildlife, cope with avalanches, or spend hours fighting unbelievable rapids on uninhabited rivers. Unfortunately, the guide who turns Expert can lose sight of the basics and can sometimes lure people into taking risks, more as a way of proving his competence than as a way of improving their recreation.

Quite frankly, the craft of guiding can in large measure be mastered by people as young as thirteen, and I've seen a few eleven year olds who didn't have much further to go. Strength and maturity are needed, but the basic skills are easy and practical enough to suit the capabilities of young or old. In part, that's what makes camping a good cross-generational activity. The basics are needed at all ages and they provide common ground for constructive group activity.

Obviously, there are fine points to any craft, but if you're looking for the exotic or unusual in campcraft, you won't find it in this book. The suggestions I offer are no more complex than those found in the Scout Handbook. My advice is aimed at simple, enjoyable camping as a shared activity. My goal is to promote safe and happy wilderness-style canoeing and camping for both young and old.

Using Nature

We did a long hard pull against wind and waves for two miles. We were at the downwind end of the lake when we started, and the wind and light rain tore into us. The bow paddler was soaked by spray off the curling waves and from the crack we made as we banged into the more solid ones. It was a tough, bumpy ride, and we had to keep on our toes to paddle through, but it was one of those cases where there wasn't much choice. Reaching the only campsite after the portage meant paddling into the weather.

Unloading was a mess too. The canoes sloshed around in the wave troughs, and we had lots of wet people and damp gear. Setting up a good camp isn't a huge problem, but it does take time. The wind kept up, but the rain quit, so we managed to get things pretty well dried out. Then the rain returned in low, scudding clouds that looked gray and raw.

A nice day had done a quick turn, but next to the tarp we had a warm area and a fire going, which made conditions pleasant enough under the circumstances. The kids were dragging in wood. After that we got a game started. A few people tried wetting a fishing line, while some of us sat around and talked in between getting things done.

Nature wasn't overly cooperative that day, but we used it to make ourselves comfortable. We also used our own interests and imaginations to improve the situation and prepare for more rain, but we used nature at its best when we sat around and talked, for what could be more natural than conversation? It's about as old as humankind. That's natural enough for me. If part of nature says, "You can't paddle today," another part suggests, "Let's paddle the social sea."

One of the nice things about being in the bush with people is conversation. People are interesting, even if they don't think so sometimes. Some of my best times have come as the result of sitting around and chewing the fat. Conversations wander around lots of topics, so it's not dull.

I like to see people as part of nature. Each one is a story of life. There are so many twists and turns in life that it can be fascinating to hear how someone has rambled along from turning point to turning point.

There is something compelling in human conversation. Some stories unfold slowly, like time-lapse photography. Others burst out quickly, like mushrooms overnight. Some open easily to the first rays of inquiry or interest. Others will remain closed until toward the end, when the person inside starts to break his own shell. Some stories are bare, wispy shoots that are green and slender. Others are formed of a massive, gnarled trunk. Both have roots that may run deep and far. Even superficial talk has roots, and sometimes new roots form from the cultivation of conversation.

Nature may prevent travel for days at a time. When that happens the human treasure may have a chance to unfold. Long after a whopper of a fish has faded to a pleasant recollection the inspiration gained from someone's life will beacon clear and strong.

The guides play a role in assisting this unfolding process. They assist when they talk about their own human lives instead of achievements. They assist when they talk of people as fellow learners rather than stupid greenhorns. They assist when they speak truthfully and listen sincerely.

At the start of a trip, campers will take a cue from the guides as to what is "proper" conversation. If the guide has first-night stories full of boastful exploits, you can be sure echoes of that will carry through the entire trip. We are, in fact, so sensitive to one another and to the dynamics of conversation and social procedure that even tiny children grasp our unvoiced rules.

How often have you said, "How are you today?" to someone only to have a brief "Fine" followed by a change in topic? Quickly, the other person will go on to talk of money matters, sports, job problems, or other exploits. Most of us have a set of "safe" topics that maintain the mask we use in routine, daily life.

Humans are such that they read the mask, respect it, work around it, and often like one another in spite of it. We read others and are read in return constantly. Some scientists claim that more than 90% of "meaning" in human interaction is drawn from nonverbal or nonspoken sources. Apparently we are very good at reading that which is not spoken and which is often thought to be hidden.

I am not going to say that masks must be ripped away. On the contrary, they are too useful in a mass society where we are overwhelmed by social input. In a rainstorm we wear a raincoat. In a social downpour we wear a mask. It prevents saturation or overload.

However, a canoe trip with ten fellow beings is not mass society. The defensive mask will relax of itself. It will remain, but it will not be as fully formed. Indeed, the social relaxation of wilderness travel helps to relieve a strain that we seldom notice because it is so much a steady part of us. We are, for a while, freed. Someone who holds a great deal of responsibility and authority carries a weighty mask, which has become himself. He knows how to direct, but he may have lost track of listening, of not having to be always on guard and evaluating. Even a slight relaxation of the mask, in that case, will yield a big breath of fresh air.

Human conversation at campfire level can nibble at masks. We all have them. Any person who hopes to be a guide must recognize his own mask, and be willing to both accept it and relax it as needed. Simplicity and personal honesty will suffice. Relaxed talk about human concerns is ventilating. The trees will not try to understand us, but we can try to understand one another. I wish to make it absolutely clear, however, that a guide's job is *not* to analyze anyone. Such analysis only introduces another form of intellectual mask and evaluation.

Analysis is not required. Psychology has little to do with it. Religious background doesn't matter. Educational level is not an issue. The guide seeks a common level based on an understanding of the human condition and sensitivity to the feelings of others.

It's as simple as saying, "I'm tired today," "Look at the Owl:" "It's cold," or "This is a nice spot." Comments should be directed at the here and now to begin with. It's pointless to go into the bush and talk about what you're missing at home. The first step of personal honesty is dealing with the immediate situation in as positive a way as possible.

Beyond comments about the here and now, the guide can refer to himself in an honest way. He can talk about his own feelings. For example, he might make a statement like, "The first day confuses me and makes me feel edgy because I'm trying to make sure I get you off to a good start. I don't want to forget things you will need to know. So, please excuse me if I seem distracted or aloof."

It's not very profound, yet, saying something like that deals honestly with the feelings and reality of the first day. The guide has opened a door. The others will see what he means. They will understand from their own base as human beings. He has said, "Here is my position as a human among you." Not a single camper will have failed to notice that the guide has seeemed preoccupied all day. The explanation will be a relief and an act of courtesy.

Analyzing first-day jitters will not change anything. Kicking it into the open at least opens the door. The appropriate action is conversation. Do not keep such feelings to yourself under the false judgement that others will not care or understand. Not only is it egotistical to think that, it also thinks for others. Just say what you're feeling and let them decide.

Commenting positively on the here and now and expressing your feelings in a simple, straightforward manner are both first steps. It may take some days of that before any broader or more personal action is needed. However, what follows will be built on whatever base has been provided. It will come naturally, and it will be a simple expansion of what has been described. It's like the growth of a seed. We don't have to provide a plan for seeds to follow. Human minds are equally fertile in following fresh, new leads.

As trust develops along with familiarity, the conversation will blossom more and more. Sincere listening helps. Many people don't get much chance to be heard. A guide can at least listen well. Listening shows respect, and it is a basic human act.

It must be clear, too, that the guide is not a performer full of tales and entertainments. There is a place for those things, but there is a place for more personal talk as well. Like the person with the strong mask described earlier, the guide must be willing to relax in his role when sitting around the campfire.

That's important, and yet it's easy to forget. But the guide who loves the work will love the opportunity for human contact that is part of it. The reason for setting aside the mask of guiding is joy in sharing life with others. There is joy is hearing other life stories. And there is joy in telling something of your own. No matter how humble it sounds to you, your story is real and vibrant with life. Sometimes you won't know how vibrant it is until others reflect it back at you.

Like anything else, the value of conversation carries into the future. A given comment or observation will stay with you for years. Long after it has been spoken, part of it lives on. Cultivation of the human spirit is not a barren, dull affair. We may never know exactly what the meaning of some situation was, but we can make use of our recognition of its importance. The meaning will grow of its own, so for now let us simply recognize the importance of the pathway that leads to fuller meaning. That's enough for a long, full trip.

Wilderness-Style and Guiding

Mention wilderness and images appear: mountains with snow-whitened peaks; rugged, forested slopes bathed in pure, cold air; miles of pine-fringed shoreline with islands like tree-masted ships. Visions of such awesome scenery inspire a special set of words, like "unspoiled," "wild," "untouched," and "pristine." The images and words we associate with wilderness often reflect an uncommon extreme, like that found in commercial movies about wilderness. (You know the kind of movie. It features a brave little family that starts from scratch and ends up with a ski chalet-type house in no time. Parents and children live off the bounty of nature and the harvest from a postage stamp garden containing soils capable, at best, of sustaining the slow growth of trees.)

In our mythical wilderness the scenery is, of course, always splendid and grand. But other associations we have with that sort of wilderness may as easily repel as attract people to a wilderness experience. Put simply, the more remote and rugged the picture, the more forbidding and impossible it seems. We are attracted to and take considerable pleasure in the awesome scenery, but in the backs of our minds there's the gnawing suspicion that the image is too good to be true.

So it is that many people who'd like to try a wilderness excursion are put off by unrealistic ideas of what wild country is like. And I can't blame them for having avoided wilderness because it looks too difficult or because they can't imagine how they could possibly cope with so many challenges, all disguised as a vacation. Sane people don't go around looking for trouble, and the average parent knows what a joy it is to put together a weekend jaunt, pack the car, get everyone going and organized, and so on. A normal vacation is plenty for most people, who just don't feel the additional need to take on mother nature for a week of "roughing it."

That's why I make a distinction between WILDERNESS (writ large and mythic) and wilderness style. In actuality, most wilderness areas are not as formidable as the rugged image of popular perception. In practice, wilderness-style recreation is easy, affordable, and constructive. It is not a matter of man against nature. It is a matter of using nonmechanized, portable, and relatively inexpensive gear and basic camping practices on simple campsites. In short, I wish to remove some of the picture-poster grandeur, some of the hype, and some of the misunderstanding, replacing it with the concept of wilderness-style recreation.

In wilderness-style camping there is a simplification of material needs. Housing is the portable tent. Meals are dehydrated for lightness and to avoid the need for refrigeration. Transportation depends on muscle power rather than petroleum. Essential needs are met, but the excess is trimmed away, making us more aware of our fundamental requirements. In such a situation one gains a bit of insight or perspective on human history, living, society, physical needs, civilization, and spirit. Strip away the superfluous and there's a trim, inviting picture.

Wilderness-style camping can appear difficult at first, and, indeed, some outdoor situations are not easy. But most of the time this kind of recreation does not require extreme effort. So long as you are in a predominantly natural, undeveloped setting using uncomplicated camping practices, you've got wilderness-style camping. It should be relaxed, enjoyable, and provide enough time and opportunity for the change in environment and tempo to be fully experienced. One way to check for wilderness-style is this: If your camping plan can involve novices, young teens, or senior citizens doing things together, then you've probably achieved wilderness-style recreation, and not an endurance contest.

I do not mean to suggest that this type of recreation is one hundred percent appropriate for everyone. Some people simply won't like it, period. Others may have physical needs or limits making it too risky or difficult. And even the best trained and experienced campers will find some days frustrating to the point of despair. A plague of no-see-ums is enough to drive anyone out of the bush, and my philosophizing on wilderness style won't make a steep portage one bit flatter.

But I do suggest that a relaxed attitude makes recreation in wild country more accessible to more people than has previously been thought. Wilderness that can be enjoyed only by mountain climbers, adventurers, and fitness fanatics is more the exception than the rule. Outdoor activity encourages fitness, but one need not be a top specimen of physical culture to participate. Indeed, if the goal is simply to improve fitness, then nearly everyone is a candidate. Wilderness-style activity is not elitist.

In my role as a guide I try to make wilderness access easy and appealing. In practice, I've used the concept of wilderness-style to give me guidelines to create plans and practices that are "people conscious." The approach I take is humane in orientation, while being equally responsible toward the natural environment. In my view, the happy mix of people, simple camping, and nature creates the best kind of living environment.

For guiding, I've carried that thinking to its logical conclusion. If I want the experience to be "re-creation" for my clients, then it must be the same for me. If I'm too pressed or preoccupied to relate as a human being, then I can't guide them toward a relaxed, personal encounter with nature, others, and self.

That's how I determined that a guide team was better than a solo guide for wilderness-style activity. With a pair of guides, clients get more and better attention. And having an assistant you know and can rely on is a huge relief for the senior guide. The combined effort of two guides provides more complete attention to detail, and this translates into a more complete experience for clients. This is especially important in the first few days when there is so much new information to present. For one guide, it's an enormous load, but two guides can share the tasks and instruction with style and ease.

All of my guiding partners have been lads in their early to late teens. And, frankly, they have been a blessing. Before most new seasons I've had to train a new partner or refresh an old one, and doing so prepares me for the coming guide season. Every new, young guide I teach reminds me to keep things clear, simple, functional, direct, and enjoyable. I've come to believe that if I can prepare a fifteen-year-old to be my assistant after only a week's exposure in the bush, then I'm probably keeping things on a highly practical level for my clients as well. The two complement one another.

There's another benefit, too. A strapping, healthy teenager has more energy than I, which comes in very handy on portages. And a young person's enthusiasm over something I've long taken as commonplace is a gift of delight, allowing me to see the Boundary Waters through the fresh eyes of youth. Plus, having a young guide along helps on those trips where we have children, and I've yet to see an adult who can't be reached by the polite, sincere, well-trained efforts of my boy-guide partners.

Actually, it works out to be quite a combination. Take an inviting natural environment, add a trained and responsive guide team supervising the use of a simple array of camping equipment and practices, then mix in the eagerness of clients ready for some time in the great outdoors; it's such a good combination that I often feel as if I haven't done a thing, that nature has simply spoken directly to each person's heart.

Canoe Design

The past decade has seen a number of design changes in canoes. Such changes are interesting and valid, but they do not have equal utility or value if applied to recreational touring. Modern canoe designs tend to favor race-like activity, though they include some seaworthy features. The sleek racers of current origin are of a different breed than the first canoe I ever bought, a much-used White boat of cedar and canvas, which frequently served to haul butchered moose out of the woods.

To tell the truth, I've a fondness for the old designs and styles, which some of today's paddlers refer to as "bruisewater canoes." Called "awk-ward," "inefficient," and "dull," the traditional canoe is a product of much development. In the old days, racing was much less important than cargo capacity; canoes were used for survival and work, their shapes representing functional compromises between capacity, speed, stability, and handling. But I have to be honest and confess that the old designs have flaws, just as the new ones do. To be fair (as well as educational) about it, I will present a side-by-side comparison of features.

ENDS

TRADITIONAL
Full-ended
Relatively low, some upsweep.
Curved, rounded.
Heavy or blunt stem piece.

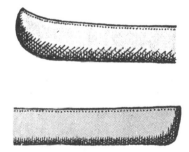

MODERN
Narrow-ended
Very low, often flat.
Sheer, up-and-down.
Fine or knife-edged hull.

(Very high ends associated with Indian and fur trade canoes have not been common for a long time. Their function disappeared when canoes came to be built of cedar and canvas or aluminum, though a few builders favor high ends for reasons of style.)

SHAPE

TRADITIONAL
Somewhat rounded.
Beamy, large waist.
Symmetrical.

MODERN
Sharp.
Narrow, tight waisted.
Sometimes asymmetrical.

With canoes of equal length and equally loaded, the modern design will provide somewhat less flotation.

SIDES

TRADITIONAL
Tumblehome most common.

MODERN
Straight or flare out.

Straight or flared sides are better because they deflect waves away from the canoe. To be honest, I never did see much advantage in tumblehome and don't miss it at all.

SEATS

TRADITIONAL
Simple bench.

MODERN
Bucket seat and foot braces becoming standard.

I like a flat, smooth bench because it allows me to shift close to the side of the canoe I'm paddling on. With bench seats, both paddlers can be off-center while maintaining a trim canoe. A fitted bucket and foot braces, however, provides much additional leverage and contributes toward a powerful stroke.

BOTTOM

TRADITIONAL
Flat.

MODERN
Rounded or arched.

A flat bottom feels stable, but once you reach the critical point of being out of balance, a flat-bottomed canoe will roll quickly and completely. A rounded or arched bottom canoe feels tippy most of the time, but it doesn't have as sharp a critical point where rollover takes command.

PROFILE

TRADITIONAL
Rockered, ends turned up several inches.
Fixed keel.

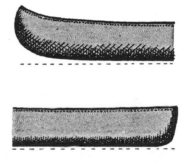

MODERN
Nearly flat, minimal rocker.
No keel.

In a modern canoe, the line of the hull in the water replaces the keel. However, the new design must sit deeper in the water for this to work. Rocker, while most often associated with making sharp turns in whitewater, is also useful for entering shallow water to land.

WEIGHT & MATERIAL

TRADITIONAL
Aluminum.
Light.

MODERN
Fiberglass, synthetics. (some wood strip)
Often ultra-light.

Fiberglass and other space-age materials can certainly be worked into finer shapes than can sheet aluminum, so new materials have opened up some design options. For all its limitations, though, aluminum is durable and practical, unaffected by sunlight or freezing, both of which can shorten the lives of some synthetics. In terms of weight, a lighter canoe will respond more quickly, but it will also be more vulnerable to winds and currents. A canoe can be too light and "bouncy," just as one can be impossibly heavy and waterlogged.

I have not, by any means, covered all the angles of design. I think, however, you can see the principle differences between traditional and modern designs. Some new elements I am in complete agreement with (such as low ends and flared sides). Other elements strike me as being moot (as in bottom shape and initial versus terminal stability—on paper it's a factor but in practice I've *never* rolled a canoe outside vigorous whitewater.) With most design changes, I see as much trade-off as I see improvement.

Let me give an example. A traditional canoe is rockered and provided with a keel. The modern design takes out most of the rocker and eliminates all of the keel, the reason being that the keel will "catch" you in rapids and isn't needed if your hull design is right. The traditional canoe, however, doesn't set as deeply in the water because it has more square inches of bottom area and flotation. Let's say that my traditional canoe draws one inch of water and has a one-inch keel, giving me a total draft of two inches. Alongside my canoe is a modern one, which has no keel and is drawing a total of 1¾ inches of water. Ahead of us is an obstruction 1½ inches below the surface. What's going to happen?

My traditional canoe will ride over the obstruction for some feet, because it's rockered. It will catch on the obstruction somewhat before midship. I'll be hung, pivoting, and have to work myself free.

The modern canoe will hit the obstruction first thing and will be swung sideways; it, too, will have to be worked free and into a route with enough water.

So, what is the difference? The difference is in how the two craft will get messed up. Clearly, in some conditions, if a ¼ inch is going to make the difference, then it's partly a matter of luck as to whether you hit a rock that's sloping off just right or just a little too high. Given almost equal draft, the traditional canoe will get hung near its center while the modern one will hit and be hung broadside above the obstruction. The most limiting factor is total draft; not keeled or keel-less; not rockered or flat. When you add paddlers and a week's worth of gear, the sleek racer actually draws a little more water than does the traditional cargo-floating aluminum canoe.

By this I'm saying that every design or option represents *some* compromise. The new breed is faster on straight runs when suitably laden. The new hulls are efficient and seaworthy. The promotional pictures show these boats handling difficult rapids and dishing out more excitement than a paddler could hope for. But keep in mind that the "sleek and efficient" hull is shown going *downstream*, just as "lesser" hulls will do, too. Let us at least dump the illusion that a hull of itself provides some magic boost in paddling ease or power. Believe in hulls when rapid courses are run *upstream*.

Yes, hull design is important, but a hull serves a number of functions, first of which is to provide a suitable platform for paddling. A good design should cooperate with the paddler's work, facilitating both control and forward progress. A super hull that proves difficult to manage isn't going to be much of a benefit if you're the one who has to paddle it.

In some respects, the situation with modern versus traditional canoes reminds me of the old argument over flush versus round-head rivets. At first glance, one would simply guess that a flush rivet will add less drag to a canoe than will a rivet that protrudes. But how much difference does it make? Can it be easily measured or is the difference mostly unmeasurable? Also, is the loss of strength associated with flush rivets worth the potential increase in speed? Lastly, how much is the "improvement" worth—fifty, one hundred, two hundred, or six hundred dollars?

What changes are really important? In part, that will depend on how you intend to use the canoe most of the time. But at what point do improvements stop being functional and simply get more expensive? Is a $1,400 Wonder-Hull really that much better than a $600 stock canoe? Is it $800 better? I've seen canoe prices shoot up, and I question exactly what people are being sold. Especially in some situations, the theoretical advantage of a specialty hull will make no practical impact on day to day travel. In the lakeland wilderness I've paddled, I've not seen the modern canoes come out being clearly better. In fact, I've found the following to be true:

1. Cargo area in the new canoes is skimpy and tight. Packs that fit easily in an aluminum canoe have to be forced. It would be best to invest in *four*, smaller, specialty packs rather than use *three* Duluth 3 packs (the old standard).

2. Bow and stern seating is lower, slightly crouched, slightly pinching at the middle. Rear seating tends to wedge a person between the gunwales, rubbing the hips. The bow seat is roomier, but the quick flare of the sides causes the lower hand to hit the gunwale, forcing a shorter paddling stroke.

3. In shallow water with obstructions, you may as well get out and carry the canoe. When laden, the keel-less canoe hits everything and is stopped dead at bow and stern. Nosing into a shallow landing is nearly impossible. When lightly laden, the keel-less canoe is prone to quick sideways slips when there's a pronounced chop and stiff side wind. Fine ends tend, too, to plunge deeply in heavy waves.

4. Slow speed performance or handling on tight bends on a river is poor. It takes brute force to pivot the hull. Maneuvers in confined spaces are more difficult to execute.

As I said, there are compromises. Excellent performance on big-water rivers and snappy runs on long, fairly straight, races comes at the expense of cargo, handling shallows, and slow speed maneuvering. In some parts of the country you can paddle a lifetime and never encounter a confined riverbend elbow or a shallows covered with food wood the beavers have dragged in. But such things do make a difference as you enter northern bush.

Let me return to something I said earlier. That is, the canoe hull is a platform for paddling. In that statement lies one of the bigger issues about canoeing. Modern hulls have tended to promote a change in paddling style. In the next chapter I will examine the two styles: Cruising and Racing.

Cruising and Racing Paddling

The biggest change I noticed in going from a traditional to a modern canoe was that I sat closer to the water in the new canoe. Very quickly this change worked to alter my cruising style, namely, the last half of my stroke was abbreviated and weakened as I was forced to bend my elbow in order to raise my hand clear of the water. In particular, I found that executing a J-stroke had to be done with my arms in a less powerful position than I was used to.

It doesn't sound like much, but sitting closer to the water makes a difference. Just ask a tennis player what it would be like to play having to cut short the last half of each swing. My paddling technique achieves power and rhythm as part of a process described by the full arc of the paddle from well ahead of my body to well behind. Ideally, I'm seated high enough above the water that my hand dropped over the side won't touch wet unless I begin to lean. In new canoes, dropping my hand over the side wet it by several inches. To use my accustomed style in a new canoe, I'd be dipping nearly wrist-deep with each stroke.

As I paddled the newer designs, it began to occur to me that the cruising stroke I was accustomed to wasn't the stroke the designers had in mind when modern canoes were formulated or evaluated. Time and again in pictures, I'd seen people in new canoes shown with the hand on the paddle grip positioned *over* the paddler's head, in preparation for a long *pull*. Whereas in cruising, my hand on the grip seldom passes anything but *level* with my shoulders, delivering a weighted *push*.

Over a period of time I tried to study the difference between these two styles. Some differences are immediately apparent, such as the amount of paddle stroke in the water. The new style with its stabbing pull puts the paddle in the water for approximately two feet, starting in front of the paddler and ending alongside. The cruising style I use keeps the paddle in the water for more than four feet.

The modern paddler has done two things with the pull stroke. One, he's eliminated what he feels is the wasted, back half of the stroke. The front portion of the stroke being the power portion, our paddler has deemed that power is the primary thing to be concerned with. Unfortunately, that's not entirely true. Two, the modern style is aimed at many power impulses per minute (sixty strokes per minute, the racer's goal). Rapid repetition of the power half of the stroke is effective for headlong speed under some conditions, but it is not an ideal system, as it sacrifices control in favor of speed.

The cruising stroke keeps the paddle in the water longer, and some of that will certainly seem like wasted motion. The cruising stroke, however, combines power and control as a blended movement. As an example, in a long, windy stretch on a lake, the cruising stroke helps stabilize the canoe during stiff gusts. Paddles in the water help to steady the canoe, much as keels would, while they continue to deliver a forward push. A long-lasting stroke combines motion and direction. Many times, I rely on the feel of the paddle in the water to tell me about current or sideforces. The experienced canoeist receives information from his paddle and uses it in a variety of ways. (I'll sometimes allow a stroke to slip into a slow diagonal draw during a gust, or turn my paddle where it will be most effective as a brake, to hold against the wind. The paddle relays information about the motion of the canoe, and it tells you when to hold and when to exert force. But, at sixty strokes per minute, a person is too busy to listen to the paddle.)

Of course, it can be argued that a faster pace will get you out of bad situations more quickly, so why not blast along with a racing style? In side-by-side situations, I've seen those relying on the racing style do little better than I. They can pull ahead, but the amount of energy they expend seems greater than what I must spend. They also work harder for control. A gust that I can ride through while pulling and holding with paddle in water will cause a racing paddler to double his efforts. And because racing paddles are out of the water more often, the canoe is actually more vulnerable to gusts. In addition, the racing style accomplishes steering by the simple method of switching sides, there is yet more opportunity for the wind to push the canoe around while the paddler takes time going from side to side. A good racing team will have worked out strategies for switching, drawing, paddling on the same side, etc., and a racing team exhibits decent control because they act in concert, but less practiced paddlers will tend to get thrown widely off course as they struggle to control the canoe.

The use of short, quick, pulling strokes is only part of the change that comes with modern canoe design. Added to that comes the use of specialized paddles. Once the new stroke is combined with the bent paddle, there is no choice—you *must* steer and control the canoe by frequently switching your paddling side. The stern steering or J-stroke can't be done as a stabbing pull with a bent-shaft paddle. Emphasis on forward speed produces faster travel, but there is a corresponding loss of control as even the *opportunity* for control is lessened.

There is nothing wrong with the pull stroke used in racing. I use a version of it myself, at times, to work upstream against a current, for example. I also use a faster repetition of my cruising stroke when a burst of speed or power is called for. In general, I use a variety of strategies to keep the canoe moving at an efficient, practical speed. (Indeed, going slowly and then speeding up makes for laborious paddling. A steady pace is more pragmatic.) So, my concern in these pages is not to condemn a particular style or option. Many different styles and strategies can contribute toward furthering a canoeist in his travels. My argument or complaint comes when a design (in paddle or canoe) begins to dictate and limit the options that will work. I can, for example, use the racer's pull stroke in my "traditional" canoe, but I can't very easily use my cruising style in a "modern" canoe. To be virtually locked into one paddling strategy is a huge limitation if your goal differs from those goals currently presented in the marketplace as ideal.

My comments about paddling are written with seated paddlers in mind, but kneeling is back in favor with some paddlers. I recommend kneeling for dealing with strong wind and waves. When you kneel, your weight is lower in the canoe and a lower center of gravity will give a steadier canoe. Also, a kneeling bow paddler ends up far forward in the canoe, making a bow-heavy boat with an apparently light stern, which will stay downwind. That is an advantage for control if waves don't break over the bow and begin to fill the canoe. I've rarely encountered conditions that required kneeling (or perhaps I've rarely ventured out under such conditions). If you are a kneeling paddler, your stroke strongly favors the pull technique using the upper torso. Kneeling, it is about all you can do. I find kneeling to be a weak, tiring, limited way to paddle.

The following sequence drawings attempt to fill in material about the paddling strokes described. On paper it's quite tricky to describe the interplay between paddler, paddle, hull, water, current/wind, co-paddler, and passing conditions (gusts or choppy areas). I've tried to suggest some of the main differences and strengths in the strokes, in as objective a way as possible. I hope this approach will be of benefit to users of both styles.

The Cruising Stroke done in a *modern* hull, with the paddler seated approx. 5 inches above the water.

The stroke begins a little sooner than in a traditional canoe, as sitting closer to the water gives less forward reach. However, the basic elements of the Cruising Stroke are intact to begin with. The lower arm is straight, the shoulders and body are twisted, the upper arm is ready to punch from shoulder-high.

33

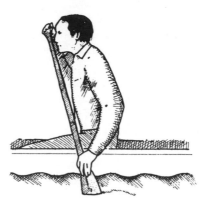

As the stroke moves alongside, it begins to be compromised. In order to clear the water, the lower arm must bend. As it raises, the path of the upper hand is raised and disturbed, too. Part of the punch is lost and the fulcrum swing of the lower arm has lost some of its flow, diverted into having to lift the paddle, which does nothing toward assisting the paddle's real work.

The Cruising Stroke is nearly back to normal at the end of the stroke, except that the lower arm is still slightly bent and less useful as a lever. Bent, the lower arm will need to be further bent to raise the paddle clear of the water. Having to lift the paddle (as opposed to swinging it) is wasted effort. The forceful twist of the body seems to have been completed, but the stroke was disrupted in the middle, which weakened the entire process.

The Pull or Racing Stroke shown being done in a canoe of modern design, paddler seated approx. 5 inches above the water.

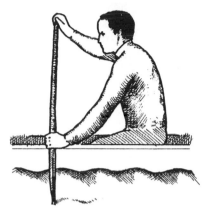

The Pull has begun. The paddler's body is leaning forward slightly and will pull back to add weight to the pull. Note the upper hand is quite high; it was even higher at the start of the pull. The weakest form of pulling with the upper hand comes at positions where the hand is head-high. The lower hand is shown using the round grip placed above the throat of the paddle. The lower arm is able to pull fairly well from a low position. Note, too, the slight bend in the elbow.

The Pull at its conclusion. The upper hand is still high, indicating a weak pulling position. The paddle has reached the paddler's chest and the paddler's body no longer leans forward. There is no place further to pull. The lower arm is bent, and will bend even more as the paddler now lifts his entire arm to bring the paddle out, clear, and back forward to begin another stroke. The hand positions one gets into at the end of the Pull are of little use for executing an efficient J-stroke.

The Cruising Stroke done from a *traditional* hull, with the paddler seated approx. 7 inches above the water.

Shown after the paddle is fully in the water and the stroke is well under way. Note that the lower arm is straight and the shoulders are twisted, part of the process of throwing body weight into the paddle's work. The upper hand is just visible above the paddler's shoulder; it is still on the *far* side of his body.

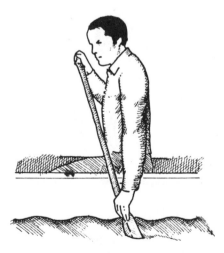

With the paddle alongside, the lower arm is still straight and the shoulders are even, having reached the midpoint of their twist. The upper hand is now forward and situated in front of the paddler, at the *middle* of his body.

Rotation of shoulders and trunk is now complete and has been delivered into the force of the stroke as a smooth and even push of weight. The lower arm is still straight and continues to act as a fulcrum. From this position, the paddler need not lift the paddle out of the water. It takes no effort to drop the upper hand, which will raise the paddle clear without lifting. Note, too, that the upper hand at the end of the stroke is not only low (at chest height) it has crossed over and is now on the *near* side of the paddler's body. (The upper hand and arm push/punch force into the paddle. The hand travels at a diagonal from far to near side and actually ends up over the gunwale on the side you're paddling. Keep in mind that the diagonal line of the upper hand and arm works in concert with the twist movement of the shoulders, allowing muscle and weight to combine for a smooth, powerful drive.)

In the previous illustration the paddle could be brought clear of the water by dropping the upper hand, or, as is shown here, the paddler could do a J-stroke, keeping in mind that the end of the paddle is very near the stern of the canoe where it makes the most efficient rudder. As shown, you see the very last portion of the J-stroke. Compare this view with the previous illustration. To executive the J, the upper hand has been pulled back toward the paddler's body and approaches his *far* side again. The lower hand and arm are still straight and have acted as a fulcrum to direct the paddle's force outward and sideways. The lower hand is about a foot from the side of the canoe, and the paddle blade would be almost out of the water at this time in the J-stroke.

The start of the J-stroke is the most powerful part in terms of steering. It begins, as shown in the previous illustration, when the paddler starts to pull his upper hand back while the paddle blade is well behind him and near the centerline of the canoe. (The stroke follows the taper of the canoe.) The first instant of doing the J-stroke is the most telling. With experience, you learn how much paddle in the water will be needed. Remember, all you need do is move the upper hand up or down and the paddle blade follows accordingly. I often drop my hand so that only an inch or so of paddle is in the water, and then I pull back to J-stroke. A shallow J, like the one just described, will send a small spray of water to the side, and that's all that's needed to cause the correction in course. A J-stroke done with most or all of the blade in the water is seldom needed.

After a J-stroke or not, the paddle is clear of the water and is swung forward to begin positioning for a new stroke. As shown, the lower hand is two feet out from the side of the canoe, the tip of the blade skimming over the water. Keep in mind that if you swing the paddle with a straight lower arm, it is never necessary to lift the paddle clear of the water with a bent elbow. (If the lower half of your paddle weighs 1 pound, consider how much weight you'd be lifting. At a leisurely 20 strokes a minute, you're lifting 20 pounds per minute. Do that for an hour and you've picked up and lifted 1,200 pounds; in five hours of paddling, a mere 6,000 pounds, or three tons.)

Note, too, that the paddle has been feathered, that is turned edgewise to your direction of travel. If you are paddling into a wind, a feathered blade requires less effort to swing forward. With a tailwind, I often let the wind help carry the blade forward, by not feathering.

To feather, both wrists are turned (there is more wrist action in paddling, than has been pointed out, but for the most part the wrist actions fall easily into line with the movements described). As long as your fingers are on the blade, you know, by feel, whether it's feathered or not—the lower wrist simply has to be cocked up. The upper hand and wrist requires a bit more explanation. The hand must open slightly and be presented in a sort of palm-up position. It then moves on the grip while it continues to pull back to the *far* side of the paddler's body, accompanied by the shoulder twist already mentioned. The lower hand will reach a forward position near the gunwale, the shoulders will be back in a twist similar to that in the first illustration of the Cruising Stroke done in a traditional hull. To enter the paddle into the water, the upper hand push/punches up to shoulder height, at which point the paddle will be fully in the water (as in the first illustration, mentioned above) and a stronger punch can be given.

Having talked of paddling strokes, it's time to look at the paddle itself. When the J-stroke is used for steering, a bent-shaft paddle is out of the question. So, what follows is information relating to the blade style, length, and other features of conventional paddles.

The most common concern is finding the correct length or size. To some extent, this question is resolved through experience as a person comes to prefer or adjust to a particular length of paddle. On occasion, I've seen a paddler do quite well with a paddle I felt was the wrong size for him. In part, the correct length is what feels good and works well.

For cruising, however, a general rule of thumb is as follows: Standing with feet flat on the floor and close together, a paddle that just reaches your chin (head held level) will be approximately right for you. If I must pick between one a little too short versus one a little too long, I will take the one that's a bit short. With inexpensive, stock paddles, the variation in size comes in six-inch increments, making it difficult to decide. In that case, simply make sure your spare paddle isn't the same size as the one you select to try. That way, you can try the spare to see if its size is better for you.

But if you like canoeing as much as I do, you'll want a better paddle and will need a more precise measurement, which is the shaft length (from top of grip to junction of blade and shaft). For this measurement, you'll need someone to help. Stand with your left hand hanging loosely at your side. Raise your right hand, as in a court of law, then lower that hand partially until it is before your shoulder at shoulder height (your elbow will drop as you do so). Cup the fingers of your right hand and have someone measure from the center of your cupped fingers to the base of the thumb on your lower hand. That straight line will be (in theory) the correct paddle shaft length for you.

The paddle I use has a blade seven inches wide by twenty-three inches long. The shaft is thirty-seven inches long. Shorter and wider blades are available, but I do not recommend the use of wide-blade paddles. Wide-bladed paddles would be useful if the object of canoeing were to move larger volumes of water, but doing so is tiring, and control has a definite new feel that takes some getting used to.

One hundred sixty square inches of paddle blade is plenty for most people, but it is not simply a question of square inches. Placing those inches in a square at the end of a pole will affect paddle proportions as well as ease of control. Keep in mind that a blade six by twenty-four inches is esier to control because more of those inches lie along or close to the axis, where control originates.

At the grip, I prefer a Palm Grip as opposed to the T-grip. The T-grip requires that the fingers be wrapped around, a position that I find more fatiguing. With a Palm Grip, the hand and fingers cup the grip, requiring little muscle effort.

Holding the Palm Grip

With the fingers wrapped over the grip for a light hold, the hand position is comfortable and gentle enough to make blistering unlikely. In essence, the paddle grip is barely gripped at all. The fingers and thumb form a pocket that holds the paddle grip. The palm of the hand delivers the actual push. Note, too, that the fingers laid over the grip help the paddler control blade position.

The relatively loose grip of the Palm style is matched by the way I hold the paddle with the other hand. The lower hand is held open, fingers resting on the blade, paddle shaft resting lightly between thumb and forefinger. The grip is light, almost like holding a bow in archery. The flat hand with its spread fingers is on the same plane as the paddle blade, so the blade can be directed by both upper and lower hands, a very useful feature.

Holding the Paddle by the Throat

The junction of shaft and blade (throat) is mated to the junction of thumb and forefinger. The spread fingers allow the paddler to pull using the entire spread of the hand over the top portion of the blade. The position is natural and can be kept for hours without feeling cramps or pain. If you "choke" or grip hard, however, you'll get some fatigue, as you would if you were to grip just the round shaft. This hand position gives a direct feel for the position of the blade and allows the force of pulling to be evenly distributed through both hand and blade.

Gripping the round shaft is more fatiguing, though it is often shown as the correct way to hold the paddle. Indeed, some paddles feature a band or grip area that extends well above the junction of blade and shaft, where I grip. Paddles with that device reflect the racing style with its pull stroke. For the pull stroke, it's easier if both hands are eighteen to twenty-four inches apart (the upper hand is often above the paddler's chin). The lower arm is no longer used as a swinging pivot that pulls in concert with the upper arm's punch, coming from shoulder-high. Rather, a limited muscle group is used—only the pulling muscles of arms and chest come into play. These pulling muscles are not only limited, they tend to be weak (do you deliver more force by pulling your hand toward you or by punching that hand outward? If in doubt, ask a boxer), and they will fatigue more easily when forced to repeat a limited motion over and over. However, at least you can see why racing paddlers paddle so fast. They have to. The only way this system works is to repeat rapidly the portion of it that has power, the initial dig into the water.

The cruising style, in comparison, uses larger muscle groups in contrasting but complementary ways. Paddling on the left side, the left (lower) arm pulls while the right one push-punches, assisted by body weight via shoulders and trunk twisting with the thrust. When paddling on the other side, the roles of the muscles reverse, giving a kind of relief. However, because the cruising style is more complete (in terms of being a full arc of motion) it tends to be less tiring, as it avoids overworking a small muscle group by having it repeat a limited range of motions. Note, too, that the cruising style I describe places considerable emphasis on control (both upper and lower hands being able to direct and control the blade), while still allowing for ample applicaton of power. If needed, I can apply power with a pulling segment early in my stroke, or I can give a burst of power toward the end. That kind of flexibility is missing in the racing style.

In racing styles, efficiency comes by maximizing the powerful dig, by repeating the *pull* at the start of the stroke.

In cruising, efficiency comes through using muscle groups and body weight to deliver a more measured, steady flow of energy, which is constantly monitored for control.

You have, I am sure, noticed how a discussion of paddles turned into an exposé about paddling styles. I'm not trying to be disorganized, but I can find no way to separate the style of a paddle from a style of paddling. A simple change in paddle grip, for example, signals a corresponding change in paddling style. The paddle, paddler, and style of paddling all come together in a sort of interplay directed at meeting a particular set of circumstances. Slight changes can trigger subtle shifts in that dynamic process.

But let us return to the paddle. The one I use is made of native Minnesota cedar. It is very light in weight and has a bit of spring in it. To tell the truth, it is just a touch delicate, but I've used it for ten years. Handmade and limber, there's something about that paddle that works for me. The Palm Grip has a little rib on it, and the blade/shaft junction has a rib, too. If you got yourself a clear piece of cedar that was two by eight inches by six feet long, I'm sure you could rough out a pattern and hand carve one for yourself. Mine has certainly held up to much use, and all it requires is light sanding and more varnish each year.

Of course, lots of new paddles are combinations of plastic and aluminum. They are strong. But some have funny-shaped grips or other features that take some getting used to. Of all the ones I've seen, only one brand struck me as being comfortable, light, and practical, that was Cannon.

Properly cared for, a wood paddle is, I think, slightly better than a synthetic one because wood has the right feel in water, the buoyancy is proper. Waterlogged, splintery paddles are not included. In fact, when I select paddles of wood, I always go for the lightest ones, as swinging a heavy paddle takes more energy than swinging a light one. Keeping wood paddles in shape requires some regular maintenance. And if you're going to pry or push with a paddle, it had better be an indestructible aluminum one. If you *must* push with a wooden paddle, reverse it and stick the grip end down to push along the rocky bottom.

Having come this far on the topic of paddling and paddles, I have a few additional paragraphs to add, but they don't exactly fit into a particular place. So, the following is presented as general information related to paddling:

Poling. In wild rice beds, we pole the canoe using a duckbill equipped pole. An alternative to that, and also intended for muddy bottoms, is a pole with a Y-crotch. For soft bottoms, you want a pole with a larger surface area on its working end. For poling a stream with a hard, rocky bottom, you'd want a slimmer end, and you'd want it shod or weighted to cut down on wear and tear. Now, all the ins and outs of poling can't be covered here. First, it's not a big topic in my mind, and, second, you learn to pole and steer by doing it—it's not real easy to explain. However, on occasion a paddler can benefit by knowing a little about poling as it relates in general to control of the canoe.

If you are in a canoe alone and attempt to pole into a current or wind, one thing will happen time and again. You will begin to make some progress as you stand in the rear, but because the bow is high and light, either current or wind will swing the *light end down*. That's the rule. It cannot be violated. You can make progress in a trim (level floating) canoe or by going into that current or wind by working from the heavy end, which becomes the bow. Let me illustrate. You're standing in the stern and a gust has caught your bow and swung you right around. You are now standing with your back to the wind. Simply turn your body to face the wind and continue poling.

Bow Paddling. Most of my commentary has been concerned with stern paddling—I seldom address much thought to conditions in the bow. I don't think I'm unique in preferring to paddle from the stern, and over time I've come to discover why I like the stern better. It's not just the matter of being in control. That's only part of it.

Bow paddling is harder to do. Good bow paddlers are rare creatures. I'm not as good in the bow because I'm not a good enough paddler to handle it. What does it take? First, the stroke done in the bow is somewhat shorter, because the path of the paddle contacts the flare of the sides. My problem with paddling up front is that I keep raking the side of my hand or catching my thumb on the gunwale. Both are painful little habits. A good bow paddler is skilled enough to avoid that by terminating the stroke at the right time. A good bow paddler, then, will put out more strokes than will the stern paddler, who will use a longer follow-through. Second, the bow paddler takes all the punishment when the going is rough. Spray off the canoe's bow hits the bow paddler's face and body. In a rapids, the bow person will be blamed for not seeing obstructions or hazards in time. Even if the weather or water are fine, the bow paddler still gets it from the boredom which comes up there, as he's expected to doggedly plug along, ignoring the headache-producing glare that comes off an unpainted bow plate in the sun. Bow paddling is not easy.

On trips, we usually rotate so that each person paddles stern one day and bow the next. You don't have to guess which days I look forward to. And I'll tell you this, a good paddling team always remembers there are two ends to a canoe.

The Paddle Wiggle. Having just pointed out the value of having a good bow paddler to keep the canoe cracking along, I can go on to tell about something I discovered in the stern, something I would not have had the opportunity to pursue had it not been for the consistent effort of my bow paddler. Oddly, though, I don't quite know what to call my discovery. I call it the Paddle Wiggle, because that's what it is. For most minor steering corrections in the past, I'd used a weak or shallowly done version of the J-stroke. The weak J-stroke corrects for the natural tendency of the bow to turn away from the side on which the stern paddler is working. This is no fault of the bow paddler. The stern stroke simply has more ability to turn the canoe, so when you are paddling on the left, the canoe will slowly turn right. When you paddle on the right of the stern, the canoe will arc off to the left.

It was second nature to correct for this on almost every stroke with a flicking, partial J, or on every other stroke with a quick but weak J. Then, one day, I wiggled my paddle at the end instead of making a J-stroke prying motion. The wiggle was, in fact, a rotation of both wrists, which wobbled the blade back and forth three or four times. The canoe straightened out when I did that. I've experimented with it under a variety of conditions, and it always seems to work where minor corrections are needed.

The Paddle Wiggle is done quickly, and it takes less effort than does a J-stroke. As if by magic, the wiggle seems to cause the bow to go back on course, I have no idea why. Perhaps the wiggle is like that of a fish tail. Perhaps it somehow works via the canoe's inertia. At any rate, it does work and is rather fun to toy with, when conditions allow.

NOTE: I have recently learned it is possible to do a form of the J stroke with a bent shaft paddle. Time does not allow me to elaborate, but the bent shaft J stroke is done closer to the paddler's body and uses chest muscles instead of follow through and arm muscles. Though it works it seems to be a demanding form of exercise.

Spring and Fall Canoeing

Each spring there is a sudden rash of accidents and drownings as people rush to a favorite spot to face nature. High water levels from spring runoff make mild rivers into wild spectacles full of challenge. The "ultimate challenge" may be the last thing a person sees on this earth. The desire to get back into the bush after being cooped up during the winter can and often does overpower better judgement.

Cold water, whether encountered in spring or fall, is dangerous. It is able to cripple a body in minutes. Muscle function is lost rapidly, so people in cold water quickly lose the ability to move or grasp a rope. If the water is moving, the heat loss and crippling effect are accelerated. It's deadly. In cold water, a simple dump that would be little problem in summer can drain a canoeist of energy. The more avid canoeists and kayakers wear wetsuits and are aware of the dangers of fast, cold water. Yet these people die as frequently as the novice who blunders into a spring torrent unprepared for wild water.

People like me are sometimes accused of taking the "fun and challenge" out of sport. Perhaps so. I simply am not attracted to whitewater sports. I've spent years in the bush, and feel little temptation to risk equipment, life, and limb in rough water. I've found no practical reason for doing so. As far as I'm concerned the goal is to survive and enjoy the experience of wilderness travel. Fighting mad torrents of water is less than relaxing. And I remind myself of the bottom line, which is that it is not fun for me or anyone I know to attend a funeral. I do not want to go through life remembering that some flippant overconfidence on my part helped bring about a tragedy.

The whitewater lovers have assured me that with proper instruction, equipment, and experience it is safe and enjoyable. Maybe so, but I continue to place the value of life over sport.

As I've said, fast, cold water is dangerous. A minor accident is no longer minor when it takes place under life-threatening conditions. However, the problems encountered in spring and fall travel are more than just a matter of water conditions. Colder air temperatures and periods of sharp weather or storms make camping more difficult. One must consider the total load being experienced—we only have so much energy per day, and overreaching can lead to problems in stamina and judgement. Few people want to admit to something as weak and human as being tired, yet doing so is a key to survival. Difficult conditions are best faced when reasonably fresh, and knowing when to stop is a necessary part of safety.

I'm inclined to reduce travel in spring and fall by nearly forty percent under what I'd consider in the summer. Partly I do so because the camping conditions are more demanding, and I also want some spare time in case the weather is nasty. Allowing six days for a four-day trip enables one to make up time lost due to poor conditions.

The physical drain that results from exposure to colder temperatures is considerable. The wind has a great impact, and there is danger of hypothermia. A gradual decline in bodily performance and thinking is just as serious as a rapid decline resulting from dumping over in an icy rapids. Keeping reserves up is important.

Those of us who have used aluminum canoes in cooler temperatures know that a lot of heat loss goes from the body through the aluminum seat. The poor body tries to warm up the aluminum, which swiftly passes the heat · to the air and water. In this exchange, the advantages are all with the aluminum and the elements. Your body will never win. So, a piece of ⅜-inch ensolite on the seat will serve to insulate the body. I don't like thick padded seats because they raise the center of gravity and make a canoe tippier. Also, the ensolite pad will not hold water. A worn or damaged ensolite sleeping pad can be salvaged to make the seat pads, and these can be tied or taped in place.

For spring and fall trips I include an extra rain tarp as well. This will give more protection to campers, as it can be used with the other tarp to form a large wind and rain shelter. After a day's travel it is nice to be able to relax, even a little, out of the elements.

The other equipment for spring and fall trips consists of additional clothing. An explanation of what is needed follows:

Hat. A stocking cap is easy to pack, and it will reduce heat loss from the head. It can also be pulled down to protect the ears. The stocking cap can also be used at night while sleeping.

Gloves. The main problem with gloves is keeping them dry. Once they get wet they will be awfully cold to wear. Rubber kitchen gloves, if they fit well, can be used, and they do keep the wind off the skin. If cloth gloves are used, several pairs should be brought along, and wet gloves should be dried in the evening.

Vest. An insulated vest that will stuff into a small sack is good. The hollow insulations work well because they are efficient even if they get wet.

Long Underwear. At least one set should be brought. If you know it's going to be cold, then make it two; one to wear and the other to carry. Try to keep them dry, because they are awfully hard to dry out in the bush. If you're going to do any amount of packing, a smooth top will help prevent chafing where the straps ride. Long underwear can be used as sleepwear.

Foam Pad. Closed cell ensolite, at least ⅜ of an inch thick, is needed. The ground will be cold, and it takes a lot of body heat to warm up the earth. The pad should be fullsized, and I'd suggest three four-foot by two-foot pads for two people. That will give a six-by four-foot sleeping area.

Jacket. Using a wool shirt with a jac shirt may work out, and one has the option of adding a vest for extra insulation or a rain jacket for wind protection. Any jacket should fit comfortably under the rain jacket. A jacket that is long enough to partly cover the rear is best, but it should not be longer than the rain jacket.

Socks. One or two pairs of extra wool socks will help. If it's cold and rainy, warm dry feet will make a big difference. Save one pair for use at night. Take advantage of any opportunity to dry socks.

Misc. Some people like to use cold weather creams, similar to what football players use. Chapstick is also a likely thing to include. A sheet blanket liner in a sleeping bag will add a few extra degrees of comfort with little additional weight.

Wet-Foot—Dry-Foot

Did you know there are two breeds of canoeist, the wet-foot and the dry-foot? There is an interesting difference between the two groups. I'll tell you the characteristics of a wet-foot canoeist.

The wet-foot believes the loaded canoe should never touch shore. People must step out into the water, unload the gear, and then bring the canoe in. Only an empty canoe should ever touch shore. This, I've been told, reduces wear and tear on the canoe to a huge degree.

Now, for my part, I'm a dry-foot. I don't ram the canoe into shore, but I nudge that bow in tight enough so the bow paddler can step onto shore and keep the feet dry. It's not serious abuse to the canoe, and it keeps paddlers in better condition. I don't like having wet feet, and I doubt that it does much for anyone's enjoyment, so I'll risk a little abuse of equipment to eliminate some abuse of people.

The wet-foots have told me I don't dress properly for canoeing. I should wear jungle boots or sneakers without socks. Also, one is supposed to wear shorts so the long pant legs don't get sopping, too.

Of course, a person does not have to dress for wading if you don't do the wading in the first place. I don't like shorts because they leave the legs exposed to insects and brush. As for footwear, I can hardly think of anything less enjoyable than carrying a portage with wet feet. The socks crush way down and the foot squishes around, while the water tenderizes the skin and makes it vulnerable to every little shock or pinch.

I'll admit freely enough that a wet-foot canoeist looks pretty rugged and daring. They plunge into the water with real style. The macho component of being a wet-foot appeals to both sexes, too. But however rugged it may seem, in a few days it looks more like ragged. The legs take quite a beating, and you know how appealing it is to look at someone's battered, dirty legs. I know I don't look that rugged, but at least I don't have to pay such a price.

The other thing I don't like about being a wet-foot is the amount of water each wet foot brings into the canoe. After a while, the interior of the canoe gets messy and dirty. It's even worse when the water gets on the bottom of the packs, and you've got a wet blob pressing on your back over a portage.

Now, wet-foot canoeing is pretty popular with organized youth groups. I'll tell a bit of a story. I was sitting out a blow in an exposed place when another group rounded the point and saw the fury on the lake that held me back. They came into shore, and in true wet-foot fashion each paddler jumped into the water before the canoe touched. They pulled up and stood around shivering in wet feet and shorts, while the wind roared by.

After repairing inland, the group built a fire to warm up. Wet and cold, they decided that maybe it would be a good time to eat, perhaps continuing on toward evening if the wind died down.

I think you'll see that the advantages of being a wet-foot canoeist depend on unpredictable conditions. If the weather is warm and sunny, well it makes a little sense. When it's not nice out, then following the wet-foot style has less going for it. In my opinion, the important thing is to dress sensibly for any conditions, and not for an arbitrary style of canoeing that for some unknown reason assumes that tempered aluminum is as fragile as an eggshell.

It frustrates me that people get into such mindsets. Aluminum canoes aren't abused in a careful dry-foot landing. The wet-foot style puts the abuse on bodies, and I think that's a mistake. A person doesn't go into the bush to suffer, at least I hope not.

Whether it's nice out or not, having wet feet is a partial drain on bodily energy. The body tries to stabilize temperature, and it works to do that automatically. Having large areas of skin exposed to the sun is likewise an energy drain. The body will work to speed up cooling. If the weather is cool, then the body will work to increase heat.

No matter how you cut it, protecting the body from too much wetness, heat, or cold is practical. It's what clothing is all about. If it were a good idea to have mostly bare skin, animals wouldn't have fur and birds wouldn't need a feathered covering. It's that obvious. We are warm-blooded creatures. If we were small, cold-blooded creatures, the wet-foot style would be perfect. But we are not. It seems realistic enough to keep that in mind.

I won't go so far as to say the wet-foot style is silly. I'm willing to let people use the style they wish. But I do want to make it clear that one can stay dry and comfortable. Doing so improves performance over the long haul, and in my book, that's what counts. I do not want to get tired out so that by late afternoon I'm getting crabby and irritable and my decision making is poorer.

I'm content to plod along as a stodgy old dry-foot canoeist. It's not very romantic or rugged, but I can enjoy what I'm doing that way. Even a raw day has its beauty, and it's easier to see and enjoy it if you aren't shivering.

Dry Boot—Dry Foot

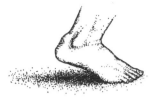

Having expressed a prejudice for keeping my feet and boots as dry as possible, I'd like the reader to consider the merits of portaging with dry versus wet feet. The advantages are especially obvious to a guide, who frequently makes multiple trips over a portage. On those days when rain pours down, the feet suffer in two ways. The first occurs because dampness softens the skin, making it tender, while the second devilishly follows, because the same dampness cancels out much of the cushioning power of socks. The feet take a beating under such conditions, and I've never found a good reason to encourage people to wet their footgear or wear soft, padded footwear that will hold water and dry slowly. For myself, I've had the best luck with Red Wing, Irish Setter Sport Boots (style 875-1), which are unlined, cover the ankles, and are flat bottomed. An unlined boot will dry more quickly and it gives body heat a greater chance of driving moisture out. Also, switching to dry socks makes damp boots tolerably comfortable.

But what's the best way to waterproof boots, you ask. After all, properly treated leather will hold less water and be more comfortable. Years ago I used conventional boot oils applied *very* heavily and very often to thoroughly saturate the leather. When wet, such treated boots felt quite slick, almost like rawhide, and they did not, unfortunately, stay as dry as I'd have liked. In fact, it seemed to me that you *could* mix oil and water, if you did so in a leather boot. Once soaked, a pair of treated boots were on a par with untreated ones. Indeed, if anything, treated boots seemed to dry a little slower, as if the oil that kept the boots secure from moderate damping trapped water trying to evaporate out.

Then quite by accident I became aware of a substitute for boot oil. A carpenter I knew told me about a cement additive which was a water repellent that wasn't oily. That's how I began to use Thompson's Water Seal® on my boots. It is a petroleum product with a sort of waxy content that penetrates deeply into leather. The petroleum distillate evaporates, leaving behind the wax. Boots treated this way are lighter than oiled boots and they are more waterproof. On new boots, I apply one coating with a stencil brush each day for four or five days. This calls for a liberal application each time, and I apply enough to leave the surface damp. Make sure all the distillate has evaporated before wearing; a full day in a warm, airy location will insure complete evaporation.

After the initial treatment, boots require only periodic applications to insure complete waterproofing, especially around the sole and seams. I give my boots two coatings prior to the start of the camping season and usually do so again at midsummer or prior to the fall season, depending on how many trips I've had. There is another advantage to this waterproofing method, too, and that is it doesn't make boots as chilly in colder temperatures. Oiled boots are notorious for being cold and stiff as a board in the chill of fall or winter. Water Seal treatment avoids that problem, and there are similar products for leather which are non-oily. One is called Sno Seal©. Others feature silicone in their content, but I'm more impressed with products that rely on waxlike compounds. I now treat all my summer boots, mitt shells, the leather tops of rubber-bottom boots, etc. with non-oily Water Seal, and the results are far better than what I used to get with boot oil.

One last note. When I talk about boots for canoeing I am often accused of being old fashioned for insisting on "heavy old boots" instead of "light, cozy canvas shoes." When I'm in the bush and it drizzles for three days running, I'll take my boots every time over tennis shoes, which are "cozy" only as long as they are kept dry. I prefer boots, in part, because they function better under the worst conditions. And even if light canvas shoes were sturdy, quick drying, and able to keep water out, I'd still want the added support of a firm leather boot, which can be snugged around the ankle. In portaging, the strain of packing a twenty-five to forty percent increase in body weight rests most heavily on the feet. A substantial boot provides a stable crepe sole, which will carry that additional weight on a firm foundation. Canvas shoes are simply not designed to deal with carrying extra weight on rough surfaces. But perhaps most important is support of the ankle joint. The advantage of ankle support becomes apparent when you consider that portaging a canoe places considerable weight overhead in a position that makes balance tricky, especially on rough ground. Carrying the canoe, you have approximately seventy pounds overhead, and while you are concentrating on the trail, an unseen branch may suddenly deflect the canoe, its weight, and finally you. The shock of a wrench like that is often borne in large measure by the ankle joint alone, and that makes a boot with ankle support a truly sensible piece of equipment. My runner friends assure me they are in such good condition that they can handle trail hazards, but realistically, I don't see how conventional exercise done on good ground prepares one for the extreme forces encountered on a treacherous portage trail. I'm convinced that the right piece of equipment (namely sturdy boots) is the key to dealing with the extra weight and difficulty of portaging. However, once the portage is over I'm not in the least adverse to loosening my boots at the top to allow greater ankle flex and more ventilation while I paddle. Or if the flies will allow it, I'll even remove my boots during paddling, thus enjoying the lightest, driest footgear of all.

Pack Rods

A beautiful pack rod, like a Trailmaster from Wright McGill, deserves good care. I get attached to any piece of equipment that holds up year after year, and I like treating equipment properly. That's especially true of pack rods, because they are so convenient for wilderness travel. Every time I use one, I feel good about the equipment, its fishing history, and about having given it good care.

It's not hard to do. Proper treatment of pack rods is mostly a matter of common sense. The Trailmaster rods come with an aluminum tube and cloth liner. The liner should be kept dry. After a rainy spell in the bush, I spread everything out in the sun for a half hour. That keeps the interior surfaces of all equipment dry and clean. After each trip rods are likewise spread out inside so they can be dried and checked.

For most people, the main weakness with a trail rod is getting the parts and pieces together properly with a minimum of wear and tear.

When I put a rod together I start from the tip and work down. That keeps the rod light and easy to handle while being put together. I loosely line up the tip pieces and sight down the guides to line them up. When that's done I push the sockets together firmly to seat them all the way. After doing that, it's best to check the alignment again. Careful twisting can correct slight misalignment. As pieces are added, the same procedure is followed until the handle is put on.

Many times people will start with the handle and then end up fighting its weight as the rod goes together. That's awkward, and it may distract a person from properly seating the sockets, which is important. The sockets of each piece should be fully seated.

When I take a rod apart I work from the handle end. The easiest way is to do a half-squat while holding the rod horizontal behind you. One hand goes on either side of the first socket. The hands are in the crooks behind the knees, and the knees are maybe a couple of inches apart. Hold onto the rod firmly, center the socket between the knees, then spread the knees apart. The legs do the actual pulling apart, and the hands position the pieces while the stronger leg muscles work.

You can keep that basic position and use one hand to hold the pieces as they are separated. It makes quick work of taking pack rods apart, and it delivers a straight, strong pull that is not apt to harm the rod.

Using arms and hands in front is harder because they tend to pull at a slight arc, and those muscles don't have the strength of the legs. I've seen people damage or distort a socket with an arced pull, so it is a good thing to avoid.

Likewise, having two people pull is awkward, and many times I've used my legs to separate pieces that two people had been tugging on with little success. The steady position and strong pull from the legs will do the trick almost every time.

Last, I keep all sockets dry. Oil on socket parts only encourages dirt and grit to stick to them. Dry sockets are best, but one could use a dry lubricant in the case of sticky sockets.

Pack rods do a fine job in the bush, and just a few little tricks help them to keep on doing it.

Canoe Country Weather, a Descriptive Terminology

Shortly after I'd begun taking people on canoe trips, one of my clients, a man from California, assured me that he'd seen a year's worth of weather during our six-day trip. Since then, I've made a few trips to the West and have found, indeed, that one can go for days at a time and see nothing but clear, open sky. To many people, clouds are somewhat unusual, and they aren't used to having the weather change every hour or so, as it will often do on a summer day in the Boundary Waters. It throws them for a loop when we encounter brilliant sunshine followed by a fast-moving rain squall, which is then followed by more sun, and so on.

That sort of weather is, of course, quite easily described. We call it "quick-changing rain squalls." But there are other conditions more subtle, more difficult to capture in a phrase, and it is for these typical yet elusive weather conditions that I have evolved the descriptive terminology that follows.

Frog. Froggy weather is a composite of fog and very light (mistlike) rain. The condition is most often characterized by fog (clouds at ground level) and still air. Occasional rain drops are small and scattered. Smoke from your campfire will rise straight and slow. On a really froggy day you'll hardly know the sun exists.

Frain. Frainy weather is frog with a bit more rain. Again, there is little or no breeze, heavy overcast, soupy conditions. If you're under tree cover, frog may trick you into thinking it's frain, as mist accumulates on leaves and needles and then drops off as light rain. The effect is the same, but the condition is different. Frog can, however, sometimes quickly turn to frain. You can even create frain yourself by shaking trees on a froggy day.

52

Scud. Scud is gusty or windy frain that comes in patches. Usually the overcast is partly lifted and ground level is clear. Scud often blows along at tree-top level. In a predominantly overcast sky, scuddy patches will hang low and sail past, carrying mist and scattered rain. Scuddy weather is reasonably miserable, unless you enjoy being cold and damp.

Snert. (Sometimes called Snart) Snert is very gusty scud. It's sharp, brisk weather with winds strong enough to make paddling difficult or ill advised. With snert, though, there may be real breaks in the overcast. A bit of sun will peek down just long enough to encourage you, right before delivering another wet, snert blast. The mist-rain driven on snerty weather excels at infiltrating rain gear, and it's often blowing hard enough to sting exposed skin. When it's snerty out, you'll wish it wasn't.

Frizzle. Frizzle is a spring and fall version of snert, but it is an extreme form. With frog, frain, scud, and snert, daytime temperatures are in the 60's to 50's. Frizzle tends toward the 40's or colder. Frizzle is a great teaser, too. A cold, windy day will suddenly break open and the sun will begin to warm and dry the earth. You'll feel sure the weather is going to clear. But coming over the hill behind you will appear square miles of sun-destroying snert, blowing in with a vengeance. The blast will start with mist and move quickly to rain or even a brief downpour. It's frizzle for sure when you hear the tinging of sleet pellets hitting your overturned canoe. It's the sudden turn toward freezing that really makes frizzle, and it's not unusual to spot snow-flakes. It's cold and wet when it frizzles, cold enough to see your breath. It gets worse as darkness comes, and frizzle can become an overnight blizzard. Local tradition has it that the only way to stay warm on a frizzly day is to stay in a hotel. Good advice, but, unfortunately, not a practical solution.

Canoe country weather is full of surprises. Odd mixtures of conditions aren't uncommon, and the variety is oceanic. I once saw a "perfect" day turn into a violent midday windstorm that produced more whitecaps than I'd ever seen. The whole transition from normal to violent, back to normal took less than an hour, with only a larger number of broken trees left behind to serve as proof of its having occurred at all.

Come to think of it, I have to agree with the guy from California. I may be somewhat used to our weather, but I can recall a few times when it sure *felt* like I'd been hit with a year's worth of weather in a six-day trip.

Axe and Fire

"Leave Your Axe at Home" is becoming a frequent admonition from Forest and Park Services, as well as various volunteer organizations. Wilderness users are counseled not to take an axe and to use either downed wood that can be broken or camp stoves to meet their needs.

In many cases you can find enough small wood lying around to build a fire, so an axe *could* be eliminated. And if you carry a camp stove, then it won't be a disaster when you hit a campsite where small fuel-wood is extremely scarce. If you're prepared, an axe is not an absolute must, but I still bristle at being told to leave it behind, and my axe goes along on every wilderness trip in canoe country.

I've no desire to be stubborn on the topic. Over the years, I have seen more than my share of hacked-up campsites, the result of unthinking axe use. It's not pretty. Trees are injured and left vulnerable to insects and disease. Campsites are slowly denuded and left overexposed to erosion while providing less protection for campers. Half-chopped trees create future hazards that may crash down unexpectedly in a windstorm. Latrines and camp areas look abused and scarred. It's a shame, and it is true that if axes were eliminated, then much of that type of destruction would be eliminated, too. But I hate to see the innocent tool take the blame.

And though I don't like to see campsites degraded by senseless destruction of trees and ground shrubbery, there are some benefits to the environment when wood is gathered, cut, and burned. The litter of wood chips from chopping and handling wood leaves behind natural debris which, to some extent, deposits an organic covering, preventing soils in campsites from compacting. Every time campers bring in wood, they re-litter portions of the surface, contributing toward campsite stability. Visitors of a "purist" disposition see such wood chip litter as a disturbing sign of human presence, but during a downpour I'd rather have raindrops hitting woody litter than bare, unprotected earth.

When I go into the bush, I take my axe, and it gets frequent use. Its main purpose is not, however, to chop things down. Most of my cutting is done with a folding camp saw. Properly set (I use blades with a deep, chip-clearing gap every third or fourth tooth, and I use a saw set to get a wider-than-normal cut), and kept sharp with a file, a saw is much more efficient than an axe. Dead trees are sawed to convenient lengths in the woods; these pieces are then hauled into camp to be further cut to burning length.

The axe comes into its own for *limbing* downed trees and for *splitting* firewood. Being able to split wood is particularly important for fires in rainy weather when the only dry wood will be *inside* a log. Being able to provide fire and heat when it's wet and miserable contributes to the health and safety of campers. However, on my trips, no camper is allowed to use the axe.

The guides are the only ones allowed to handle the axe, and in this way we prevent injury to inexperienced people. Learning to work with an axe takes time, and I figure that my clients can learn those skills in another setting. After all, one glancing mistake that results in the axe entering your leg or foot and your vacation is ruined.

In the following pages I will present some information on using the axe. But such ability cannot be learned by reading. These tips will only serve to provide a few pointers.

For an axe, I use a three-quarter axe with a Hudson Bay or Scout Pattern head. The heads on these weigh approximately 1½ pounds. True Temper, Plumb, and Kelly all make quality axes and can provide substantial sheaths (a real necessity). I trim off the pointed fawn foot on handles, then sand smooth the end. Handles need to be inspected and cared for regularly, and I've found boiled linseed oil is good, routine treatment. A slightly loose handle can sometimes be cured by an overnight soak in linseed oil that was first warmed to one hundred degrees or so. The following day, wipe off all excess and allow to dry for another day or two. Don't allow a wet sheath to stay on your axe for days at a time. Separate the two to facilitate drying. I oil my sheaths at least once a year, which keeps them supple and extends their lives. Keep the cutting edge of the axe sharp by filing with a medium file (bastard file if the edge is bad). If you've hit a rock, be prepared for more filing, because the rock strike will compact (work harden) the metal and leave a hard, dull spot on the blade.

My axe is carried on the outside of an equipment pack to which I've added two loops and a strap. This simple arrangement allows easy access to the axe in the event it's needed to clear windfalls on a portage. This system also keeps the weight of the axe low on the pack.

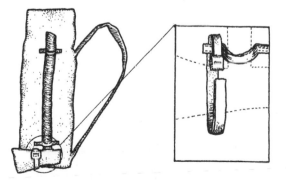

The drawing shows this equipment pack, but in showing the pack, I am faced with the dilemma of whether to deal with it now or return to it in a later chapter. At the risk of disturbing the flow of information, I'll cover the equipment pack here and now.

A Duluth No. 3 Cruiser pack is shown, but you can't see the contents of the pack nor the secret ingredient. The equipment pack is used for much of the hard, lumpy, bulky equipment; the cook kit, dishpan, tackle boxes, dutch oven, and first aid kit all go in there. Unfortunately, all those small, hard objects want to shift around in the pack, usually ending up as points at the back of the pack where it meets your back. That brings us to the secret ingredient, which is to cut a square of ⅛-inch waterproof plywood to match the back of the pack. After cutting, sand and round all edges, then follow with a good application of Thompson's Water Seal (great for waterproofing and oiling leather, too). When this plywood insert is placed at the back of the pack the small, hard objects rest against it, not you. I slip the rain tarp, plastic sheeting, or ground cloth between plywood and pack, thus providing a flat, firm, padded back. In camp, the plywood piece can be removed and used as a flat surface or as a windscreen to aid cooking, especially when using a stove.

Now let's return to the technique for chopping wood, which looks so easy and obvious. Every urban lumberjack has seen the lyrical outdoor fantasy where Ma, Pa, and the Kids live surrounded by enchanted nature. They live for a year on what grows in a tiny garden and what they gather in a few berry pails. On film, their firewood splits with a satisfying "clunk" when given the proper blow. So, our urban lumberjack winds up and take his crack at a piece of wood—the result being either an axe stuck in a subborn bolt of wood or passing through the wood and into the rocky ground with enough force to split a moose in half.

The unpracticed axeman lacks a feel for how much force is needed for a particular size and species of wood. This sense will come only with practice and experience, but placing wood (instead of rock) under the piece to be split is simply common sense. However, trying to split wood over too-soft or springy a base is as ill advised as splitting over a boulder. So, the axeman tries to select the right sort of spot, such as a sound stump or substantial fallen log.

If you've got dry, seasoned wood, it will probably *not* split as readily as green wood. Notice where the knots or branches are, and place them down, away from the striking surface, as shown. With experience, you know which end of a piece to attack and even what spots on the piece look "likely."

At times it may be best to split from the side, as shown. An alternative to this is called the Contact Method, a very safe way to split wood and one covered in the Boy Scout Handbook.

On big pieces, the inexperienced axeman will wind up and clobber the log dead center, harvesting a solid "thump" for his efforts. On large logs, one should first try to break the bark. First hit one edge, then directly across from it, and then the center. Once halved, the rest will split easily.

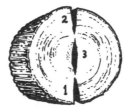

Large pieces will sometimes yield to quartering or penting, where one removes exterior slabs of wood as a first step.

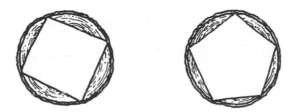

Once the slabs are removed, then the corners are attacked. In this way, big logs can be reduced to burnable size. But if the piece is full of knots or is twist/burl grained, it may not split at all.

Splitting will sometimes be easier, too, if one attacks the wood at an angle. Such a strike tends to knock a split piece *away* from the parent bolt. An alternative to this is to twist your axe handle slightly on impact, thus helping to pry split pieces free. Getting the correct timing on the twist is a slow process that requires much practice.

Yet another alternative is to reverse axe and log once the two are "stuck." Slamming this combination down will often split with one blow because Force is equal to Mass times Acceleration. The accelerated log delivers more force to the axe than would the axe to the log.

On a really wet day, your axe helps provide a warming, welcome fire. But to get there you've got to do a fair amount of work.

First comes fine, tissue-like birch bark. This is often found on the ground or hanging loosely on healthy trees from which it is being shed. Where fine tissuey bark is available, I'll often stock up and carry a supply with me. Even soaking wet, such fine bark shreds will burn readily. A small handful of this will be needed to ignite your kindling when you begin a fire on wet, cold ground.

Every fire has three requirements: fuel, oxygen, and heat. On wet ground, much heat is lost as it goes into warming the ground, so be prepared for it to take longer to get a good fire going. To get enough heat to dry and warm the ground as well as sustain burning, you've got to have an abundance of small, dry fuel. The space under Forest Service grates is often too small for enough fuel, so be prepared to remove or scrape aside some of the accumulated ash. In addition, too much wind may blow heat away from the fire faster than fresh wood can be heated enough to burn. New fires often die because someone tries to rush the process and throws big wood on an infant fire.

Having your birch bark and a cleared out space to build your fire is not enough. You need *lots* of the right kind of fuel. On a bitterly cold, windy, drizzly day it may take an hour to get a fire established firmly. That means there are many steps that need to be taken.

Start with squaw brush or fine, wirelike twigs, which are the dead, lower branches from balsam or spruce. Broken into small, fanlike piles, these lacy twigs will ignite from the heat of your bark. But you need lots of them. And even wet twigs will burn if you've enough bark to warm and dry them. However, when it's wet, add curls or shavings taken from split wood in order to mix dry wood with the twigs. That way, you insure a better burn.

Make a pile of slivers to add to the twigs and curls. Dry slivers are taken off split pieces of wood almost the way you'd remove shavings. Work on edges of wood with either a knife or the axe head used like a chisel.

Slightly larger splits should be made, too. These fine splits are nearly pencil size, and a good criss-cross layer or two of them can be added once your slivers are burning brightly. If it's quite wet and cold, several layers of fine splits will be needed before you can start to add splits approaching finger or branch size.

If your fire seems to grow weak, immediately feed it smaller fuel. Work slowly toward burning bigger pieces, and then only after it appears the fire can consume them. In bad weather, I often continue to supply small pieces to the fire in order to help it burn the bigger pieces. Bigger pieces, too, should be split, as split faces are dry and seem to burn better. When it's nasty out, your fire will require much tending, but it is a good way to keep your hands warm.

When the weather is raw, your axe is an essential tool for building a good fire. And a warm, cheery fire feels good to both body and spirit. If you included a rain tarp in your kit and can keep out of the wind, you can be warm and comfy even during the worst summer weather.

What Wood To Burn?

People from other areas often don't know our northern trees, and they are confused about what wood to burn. The following brief explanation will, I hope, be of help. If needed, doublecheck with a tree identification book.

Balsam and Spruce. These two small- to medium-size conifers often grow in tight, dense stands. In such places you can find dead, standing trees to take for fuel. Dead branches on both types of tree provide excellent small kindling. Trees of six to eight inches in diameter are common. When dead, the bark is dull, split, and the tree will have a scattering of sawdust around it from insect attacks. Trees toppled by the wind will be sound in those portions not resting on the ground. Sound, dry pieces of balsam or spruce will burn fast and hot; they are not fine producers of coals. Fine splits of either are good fire starter and kindling. If the wood feels light and spongy it's best set aside as F.W. (explanation at end of this chapter).

Birch. This is a favored wood for heating homes, as it is abundant and moderately hard, making it efficient for burning. In the bush, however, birch is seldom of use because it sours and rots so easily. After one season, a birch log with its bark intact will be spongy and difficult to burn simply from having lain on the ground. Birch is excellent firewood when it's been *cut, split*, and allowed to *dry*. Obviously, it's rare to find wood lying about in that condition. If your axe feels like it's hit a firm melon when you try to cut or split a piece of birch, you may as well consider that you've got yourself some F.W.

Aspen. Dry aspen is good fuel, and greenish aspen will burn well once you've got a hot fire. Gnarly aspen branches from dead, standing trees are good kindling after you've got at least half a start on your fire. Aspen will remain sound or burnable even after a few years of lying on the ground, because its bark will split and shred loose in black, sick-looking patches that allow moisture to leave the log (exactly what tight birch bark does not do). Like balsam and spruce, aspen is not an excellent coal producer and will burn away to feathery, white ash. A potential source of dry aspen (and birch) for fuel comes from beaver cuttings, with all the bark having been eaten off. If it's out of the water and exposed to the sun, barked aspen and birch will stay sound for years and can be picked up along shores where beaver work.

Pine. Both red and white pine are fairly common, but these species get rather big to be a handy source of fuel. However, the branches of toppled pine are fine for burning because they are of a convenient size for handling and are quite dry. (The surest sign of a dead, dry pine or conifer is when all the needles have fallen off. Trees with all brown needles are dead, but still moist inside.) If bigger pieces are available, they will burn best if split, thus exposing the inside wood to flame without the protection of the slightly fire-resistant bark.

Cedar. If the weather is truly nasty, wet, cold, and windy, I look for dead cedar for getting the fire started. This aromatic, rot-resistant wood makes fine shavings and delicate, tiny splits. The shaggy bark will usually slip off dead trees, promoting dry, sound wood. Because it is a light wood, even cedar driftwood is often burnable, especially those portions exposed to the air. I've found entire drift logs of cedar, which I sawed up and burned for fuel many years after they'd been cut down.

Other. A true hardood is rare in the north, and I can only count a few times when a type of wood other than the above was of use while camping. Looking at the list, you may wonder how we sustain a fire up here, lacking fuel that will hold coals for hours. The answer to that is stumps and knots of pine. Small stumps can be ripped out of the ground. Larger ones can be sawed and split on site. What you harvest is gnarly or twist-grained pieces, rich in resins. Conifer and pine stumps remain visible because they are preserved by oily resins. If most of a stump can be kicked into powder, there will still be resinous portions of it that will burn eagerly. You may spot the line of a huge, fallen pine in the forest. The mound of its decayed trunk may be covered with moss and small plants, but if you break open that soil, you will find intact pine knots inside. Those knots will burn! The dense, oily wood of pine knots and stumps will burn long and hot, but try not to cook over them, as they are terrible soot producers and can even flavor your food with their smoke. If, however, you need fuel, this oily wood will burn even when quite wet, as each piece is soaked in its own waterproofing bath of resin.

F.W.. That stands for Fun Wood. Your best, soundest, driest, pieces of wood should be saved for cooking. This is referred to as W.W. or Work Wood. Fun Wood is everything else that can be burned up in a campfire, when you won't mind the smoke so much because you don't have to bend over the fire to stir a pot. Every campsite seems to have an ample supply of Fun Wood, which people don't burn because it's not good wood for burning. So, instead of consuming good firewood for campfires, I burn up the worst junk on the site and save myself some effort to boot. Kids are particularly well suited to finding and hauling in Fun Wood. Having a suitable heap of Fun Wood insures, too, that the wood carefully, cut, split, and tucked away under cover along with splits, kindling, and birch bark, won't end up in the evening's campfire. I always make sure I've got a more than ample supply of good wood set aside for the next day, and burning Fun Wood at night helps me keep it that way.

Sharpening Blades

Your blades are only as good as the stone used for sharpening them. I have tried all the varieties of stone commonly available, and I think my comments will be useful and accurate. The main thing is to get a good stone. Some industrial quality stones, manmade ones, are good, but often they come in very small sizes suitable for work on cutting bit edges. Most other manmade stones are soft and coarse. The average manmade variety is a poor substitute for a good, natural Arkansas stone.

Arkansas stones come in three general grades. These are

Washita. Hard, coarse stone good for fast sharpening and a sharp edge. Washita was originally a "cull" stone that was discarded. Color is varied and mottled.

Soft Arkansas. Very hard, fine stone for giving a smooth, polished cutting edge. This was the standard stone in the old days. The classic color is pure white, but Soft Arkansas can be mottled over a range from white to black. Old stones used with oil are often smooth and yellowed.

Hard Arkansas. Extremely hard, fine stone for a nearly surgical cutting edge. The classic color is jet black. Hard Arkansas is somewhat rare and costly.

A practical size for a variety of cutting edges is eight inches long, two inches wide, and one inch thick. A longer stone is nice if you sharpen mostly long knife blades. In most cases the Washita will do in the bush. Fine sharpening is something I do at home. Soft Arkansas can be used just as effectively as Washita, but it is slower. Whether you choose Washita or Soft Arkansas is of less importance than the size you choose. A small stone is harder to use. The size suggested will do the job for many years, but the stone should be protected in a small, wooden box.

Stone care is important. Keep the stone clean. I wash these natural stones with soap and water to keep the surface open. For sharpening, I use only water. Water will not clog the surface as oil will, and residue can be washed away more easily. Also, water is available in the bush, so it is far handier than oil.

With a natural stone, the grain will actually raise a little when it is wet. At least that is what it feels like. At any rate, a dry stone will feel smooth and a wet one will feel raspier. So, as far as I'm concerned, water is the natural choice for sharpening. I know that Arkansas stones are called oilstones. That's the old tradition, but your stone will perform better and last longer if you never oil it.

If you inherit an old stone of good quality it will probably have been used with oil. A fresh surface can be gained by dressing the stone on a belt sander and by frequent washing in detergent. It will take some effort to renew the surface, but a clean surface will cut much better. Likewise, a newer stone with an uneven surface can be dressed on a sander. Note that almost all

Washita stones will have some minor imperfection in the form of a small pit or fissure. As a cull stone, Washita is prone to imperfections; it's not serious.

When it comes to using the stone, first wet it thoroughly. It will soak up water, and I add more as I sharpen. Keep it wet enough so that metal particles can be floated and rinsed away as you go along.

The angle for sharpening is 22½ degrees. Most people find that a diffi cult angle to imagine. Some angle guides for sharpening are available, however, the angle can be maintained by hand. You know what the blade looks like at 90 degrees to the stone. Half of that is 45 degrees. A quarter of that is 22½ degrees.

At first, one is wobbly about holding the angle, but the body will grasp it in time. Early attempts at sharpening should not last too long, as tired muscles make the arm shaky, and the tension of sustained concentration amplifies the shake. Short sharpening sessions spread over several months will allow the motions and angle to work in. It takes time, and regular practice will help.

The motion is simple enough. Start at the base of the blade and slide forward and along the blade to the tip. Flip the blade over and do the same on the return. Work from one end of the stone to the other. Flip the blade over at the end of each stroke, and sharpen the same amount on each side of the blade. In a way it is like shaving away from yourself on the stone and then back toward yourself.

In time your motions will become quicker as the feel of it becomes secure. Also, you'll have your own angle firmly set. If you sharpen a knife done by someone else, you'll note that it will take time to adjust their angle. Each one of us ends up with his own angle, so you'll be better off if you always sharpen your own knife.

The entire process is efficient if you do not allow your blade to get too dull. Working a dull or abused blade back to sharpness may take several sessions. It's far better if a blade is never allowed to form a rounded cutting edge.

"It Won't Fit in My Pack!"

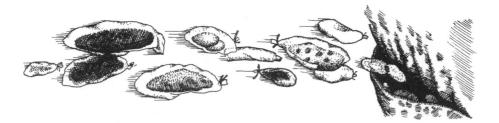

When my clients are late in arriving I often prepare for them in advance. The Duluth No. 3 Cruiser packs each get two large plastic garbage bags, one inside the other, as a double-liner. I then put the two sleeping bags into the pack, each inside a smaller plastic bag, so that all that's needed is the personal gear of the individuals.

Keep in mind, now, that I've repeatedly instructed these people to pack all their spare clothing in small plastic bags. When they arrive, however, at least one of them invariably has every item of spare clothing crammed into a single, bulky lump. He looks at the prepared Duluth pack, which seems nearly full with just the two sleeping bags inside, and he looks at his bulging plastic sack, and he looks at me and says, "It won't fit in my pack!"

And he's right. That huge lump of clothes won't fit in the pack, at least not in that condition. The cure, however, is simple. The big lump has to be broken down into small units. At home we have drawers to organize our clothing, in a pack plastic bags serve as drawers, clear bags being preferred so you can see the contents. So, the client's spare socks go into one small bag, two spare T-shirts go into another, and so on. Items that might become wet or damp during the course of the trip get separate, special treatment— swimsuit and towel each get their own bags.

These small packages are then slipped into the space between and in front of the two sleeping bags, with care being taken to keep the back of the pack as smooth as possible. You just keep stuffing those little bags in, and they keep disappearing as they get pushed into every available void and cranny. The bigger items, like spare pants, shirt, jacket go in each by themselves. In this way a reasonable change of clothing for two people for a week can fit into a single pack.

You can be sure that I often have to pare down the clothing a client wants to bring. Frequently I find myself taking the tennis shoes out of a pack, and I am all ready for the loud complaint: "What will I wear to lounge around camp in the evening?" I answer by saying, "Wear what you lounged around in all day while sitting in the canoe."

Such a response usually stops them, and it's true enough that a person will do fine with one set of footgear or by going barefoot to air the feet when it's safe to do so. But some of my clients are insistent. They want those tennis shoes along and they counter my response with the following: "Well, what am I supposed to wear when my boots are wet? I want something dry to put on my feet."

I'm ready for that one, too. I ask, "Are you going to wade in the water wearing your boots?" They *always* answer no. I smile and ask, "Then how are your boots going to get wet? They will get wet if it's raining, but what's the advantage of having tennis shoes if it rains? Your tennis shoes are less waterproof than your boots. And if you want your boots to dry properly and comfortably and more quickly, simply keep wearing them. If you keep using your boots your body heat will help dry them, and I'll bet you anything that you won't want to wear your tennis shoes once they get wet. You know how long it takes to dry sneakers, but if you want to carry around the extra weight and bulk of a wet pair of sneakers in your pack, it's up to you." Usually my clients are convinced and the tennis shoes go into the car trunk for the week.

The next battle comes over socks. Some people like to change socks once or twice a day and want to drag along five to ten pairs. I tell them to take two pairs as spares and wash out and rinse the dirty ones as we go along. Of course, they do not want to mess with doing laundry on their wilderness vacation, and they really want the luxury of having lots of clean dry socks, so they counter with this: "Well, I want extra socks so I can put something dry on my feet to keep them dry."

Again I'm ready for them. "That's a good idea," I say, "but what happens to a dry pair of socks when worn inside a wet pair of boots? If it's real wet out you just have to live with damp feet until the weather improves, because even dozens of socks won't keep up with the demand."

We have a similar exchange over flashlights, and I get them to take one flashlight per tent. (I keep spare batteries and bulbs, but it's rare that we need them.) I can get five men to agree on sharing one can of shaving cream or using soap. I can talk relatives into sharing a single tube of toothpaste or shampoo. I keep picking away, always reminding them to keep it simple and to share items where practical.

Once in a while, however, a client is a little too clever for me. I remember one woman who had it all figured out. She took along a long, fancy nightgown, intending to sleep in it, then use it as a robe in the morning—a sort of before breakfast dress. The first morning she came out of the tent wearing that thing, unlaced boots on her feet, looking very elegant. The bottom of her long nightgown dragged along on the ground, gathering dirt and twigs like an animated broom. Once she sat down she found that mosquitoes poked right through the thin fabric and others flew in under it, carrying out sneak attacks with impunity. She did not wear it the second morning.

The Handy Bandanna

What's as versatile and useful as the common bandanna? Need a quick pot holder for getting a too-hot pan handle away from the heat? Use your folded bandanna. Need a whisk to shoo the bugs away? Try flicking your bandanna. As a sweatband, throat protector, sunshade used with a cap, or handy towel for small drying tasks, your bandanna will fit the bill.

Because it performs so many tasks the bandanna takes a lot of abuse. I use mine to wipe the damp off my canoe seat before sitting down. Later I may use it to help clean my hands. Before long the friendly bandanna can become an evil, smelly rag. Fortunately there is an easy solution: soap and water.

I wash my bandanna daily, weather permitting. My usual way of doing so is to use it to wash myself in the morning, this also eliminates the need for carrying a separate washcloth. After I'm clean it's a simple matter to soap and rinse the bandanna, which I wring and then shake vigorously in order to get most of the water out. Once most of the trapped water has been forced out, it's surprising how quickly a dark-colored, cotton bandanna will dry when spread out in the sun or hung on a branch. Normally, ten minutes of drying will do it, especially if it's sunny and breezy.

Even when frequently used during the day, it's relatively easy to wash and dry the bandanna, which is always at hand in a back pocket. After toiling over a portage, I can wipe myself off with my bandanna, which has been dipped in the cool, refreshing waters of the lake. A final rinse and it can be dried, thus making it ready for another use. To be sure, it takes a bit of effort to rinse and dry your bandanna after each such use, but it's more convenient than digging around inside a pack to locate a washcloth wrapped away in a plastic bag so that its moisture won't creep into things you don't want to get damp. Keep in mind that a bandanna is fast drying; a washcloth is not.

It's been my practice to stress keeping things dry and clean, and, in part, doing so is a matter of keeping things simple. For example, when I take a dip in the afternoon I spread my clothes out on the rocks in the sun, thus assuring that my attire has been aired and dried before evening. And I don't forget the towel I dried myself with either. As soon as I'm done with it, the towel is hung in as sunny and breezy a location as I can find. On an average day the towel will be dry enough to go back inside my pack well before dark, and it should be put away before the evening dew dampens it. Attending to each detail in timely fashion will help you to be a dry and snug camper.

Of course, you can do things differently. You can let your towel hang outside overnight in the hope that it will be completely dry by the time you pack up to leave in the morning. But what if it rains during the night? Isn't it better to have an almost-dry towel in a plastic bag inside your pack than a rain-soaked towel on an outside line? Or you might be the soul who can't resist the temptation of a moonlight dip. You reason that the special occasion, its romance, etc. outweighs the fact that in the dark you won't be able to dry yourself or etc. as well as if the sun were shining. So, into the water you go. But when your dip is over and you stand on shore you soon discover that Minnesota's friendly mosquitoes know exactly how to appreciate all that exposed flesh. Rather than turn into a walking itch, you grab up your things and rush, dripping, to your tent, where the whole damp mess along with still wet you is deposited. Welcome home. In the morning the T-shirt you missed will be on the lake's edge, most likely blown into the water, and you'll find the sock that fell as you ran up the trail, and you'll curse yourself because it was from your last clean pair, and now look at it. *You* can do things differently, but as for me, I'll take comfort in wiggling my toes in the socks I've taken pains to keep clean and dry. It's my reward.

Another Handy Tip

Whenever possible I have the pair of people who paddle together also share a tent; that way their gear can stay in one personal pack, which can ride in their canoe. This system also works well for me and whoever is assisting me on the trip.

One of the functional reasons for having people who tent together paddle the same canoe has to do with raingear. It's not unusual for a quick summer rain to rip over the hills, and it's best if you can speedily don your rain suit. If, however, your raingear is in another canoe some distance away, well, there's not much you can do but get soaked. So having the raingear close at hand is good common sense.

To keep it handy, I slip my rain suit just under the pack's main flap, the one with two or three buckle straps. That way I can pull the rain suit out without having to open up the entire pack, something you certainly don't want to do if it's raining. In the past I simply slide both rain jacket and pants loosely on top, ready to be pulled out. Then one time I reached for the raingear, pulled, and watched the pants pop out with the jacket and promptly fall in the lake. I grabbed them before they sank, but I can guarantee they were no longer dry on the inside.

That taught me a little lesson. After that I always took the rain pants, folded them carefully, and placed them in one of the pockets on the rain jacket. That way the entire set was together, and there was little chance of losing the part not in use. If I'm not wearing the rain pants, then they are in the pocket. I often use the rain jacket alone, as a wind break, so this is a practical and safe arrangement.

You may think I make too much of such a small matter. After all, we are grown adults, and we do not lose track of valuable articles such as rain gear. That's what you think. One of the "lost" items I most often encounter is part of a rain suit. People take them off because they are sweaty on portages. The offending garment either gets left behind or it slips off to the side of the trail because the portager tucked it into a place that looked secure but which soon allowed it to work loose. If you are the one who has lost half of a rain suit you'll know what such a loss can mean—half a rain suit may keep you half dry, but it insures you'll be completely miserable, as well.

So, guard that raingear, keep track of it, think about it, treat it well. Today's lightweight suits are durable and effective, well worth treating with care. The biggest factor in assuring the long life of a rain suit is to limit its exposure to direct sun. I buy ones with dark colors so that they will heat and dry quickly when hung on a line or spread open. Don't leave your raingear in the sun for hours at a time. Stick close while you dry it and make sure the inside and outside get dried and aired. Then fold those pants up, put them in the jacket pocket, and put the whole thing away with your pack. I often place my raingear just inside the tent door so I can bring it out in a hurry without having to crawl into the tent.

Properly cared for, a good rainsuit will last me through half a dozen years of steady summer use. Poorly cared for, your rainsuit will leak and not serve you well, as dirt ground onto the surfce seems to quickly weaken it. A poorly cared for suit is one that takes on a distinctly moldy odor every time it gets damp. As far as I'm concerned, walking around in a moldy fog is proper reward for abusing raingear, and I hope it's one smell you'll never have to live with.

The Map, the Compass, and the User

It goes without saying that a sensible wilderness canoe trip requires good maps and some idea of how to use them. When I first began canoeing we used very general charts, called canoe country maps, which covered Quetico and the Superior National Forest. These old charts were not terribly detailed or accurate, and at most gave you a flat, bird's-eye view of the territory you were covering. But so long as you knew these charts were "loose" in terms of accuracy, you could act accordingly and be mentally prepared to find a portage in a location other than the one shown. The old charts kept you on your toes, and were quite OK, once you understood their limitations.

Maps produced by federal agencies were available then, but they were on plain paper (unsuited for the wet conditions of a canoe trip) and they were often too detailed (meaning you had to carry a lot of them), such as the quadrangle series covering only 7.5 minutes of arc. The next series covered 15 minutes of arc, which meant that on the same size paper you'd get four times as much area pictured; a handy feature, but coming at the expense of detail. What I'd often do would be to look over the detailed government maps and transfer useful information onto the canoe country charts, thus giving myself the best of both.

More recently, several firms have begun to produce detailed, handy, waterproofed maps expressly for the recreational user. The best of these are topographic, meaning they show contour lines and elevations. Because I paddle the Boundary Waters separating the United States and Canada, I have the added confusion of adjusting to two differing contour systems. The Canadians use a 50-foot interval, while the United States uses a 40-foot interval; each contour line represents a drop or rise of either 40 or 50 feet, depending on which side of the border you are looking at on your map. It sounds more complicated than it is, though, and any good book on map and compass can explain contour lines and other features to you. I will only point out here that where you see the lines get close together or very close together it means but one thing—a very steep slope or cliff.

Imagine you're on the Canadian side and your map shows four contour lines coming close together. Each line represents a change in elevation of 50 feet, so four lines close together translates into an abrupt change of 200 feet. That's quite a climb. If you find that little gem marked on a portage you just might want to reconsider your route, especially if you have to climb 200 feet UP. But how can you tell?

You can tell because some contour lines are bolder and/or they have numbers written on them. The number gives you elevation above sea level, which isn't, in practical terms, the thing that need concern you. What matters is the space between lines and whether the numbers are increasing or decreasing. When there's lots of space between lines you have relatively flat, gentle territory. Thus if the lake you are planning to portage from has an elevation of 750 (feet above sea level, usually shown on the lake along with a ⊤ symbol) and the other end of the portage shows a contour line marked 800, then you know the total climb for that portage is around 50 feet, UP. On the other hand, I can look at a map and see a trail that crosses a 1500 line and then five more lines in short succession, the fifth line being bold and marked 1250. The trail continues with lines spaced farther apart and ends at a lakeshore line of 1100. This tells me that part of the trail is steep and that the total change in elevation is 400 feet DOWN, from 1500 to 1100 feet above sea level. (The examples in this paragraph are drawn from a Canadian map, with 50-foot intervals.)

When the line you are interested in isn't marked with a number, then you simply have to count from a marked line to the one you want, adding or subtracting either 40 or 50 feet per line depending on the map and whether the contour is rising or falling.

For canoe country, however, most of what a map shows is fairly superfluous because you're not on land. The lakes you paddle will be the same, uniform elevation from one end to the other, regardless of how long or big they are. But it is nice to know in advance if your route will be going up-slope or down, and good maps will show you that information.

So, you have a decent topographic map and you know a bit about what it tells you. What else do you need to know? When you are on your trip, you have to be able to orient the map. That means you have to find the North Arrow on the map and place the North/South axis of your compass alongside it. Then rotate the map and compass until the compass needle points North. Your map is now laid out the same as the territory it shows.

Frankly, this is most awkward to do in a canoe, so if you are unsure of your territory, orient your map and yourself on land first. Be careful not to orient by placing the map over a pack with iron items in it, such as the axe. Nearby metal objects will throw the compass off. Once you have oriented the map, you can figure out where you are. From shore you can look out over the water and spot obvious landmarks that correspond to features on the map, such as points or groups of islands. While orienting yourself, make mental note of certain things, such as staying to the right of the big island you can see in the distance, for example.

70

The whole process is simple enough when you work from known locations, such as the end of a portage, or a campsite or feature that's clearly shown on the map. Keep taking tabs on your location and comparing what you see on the ground with what the map shows. This should help you avoid getting lost or confused. I keep a folded map tucked under the flap of a pack where I can pull it out and check it frequently while paddling. If I stay oriented I don't need to use the compass for these quick checks. I pause only as long as it takes to check the map against what I can see, and then I'm back paddling again. If you get lost, however, you will need to orient map and compass properly and then try to figure out where you are by looking for the most obvious, major landmarks and using them to deduce your location.

On big lakes with lots of points and islands it is very easy to get turned around. A sure method of not getting lost is to follow the mainland shore, which is usually the long, long way around. If you head into a maze of points and islands you can keep on top of your location if you take your time and check your progress often. Keep in mind that many small islands will not be shown on the map, and some massive islands can trick you by appearing to be portions of mainland shore, whereas a large point of land might look like a big island when seen from a distance. If you find yourself wandering around in a cluster of islands that all look familiar, and yet they all look strange, you can take comfort in the fact that you're not the only ones to get baffled by our more confusing lakes. It's happened to me often enough, and I've come to call these incidents "scenic excursions," because they expose a person to lots of scenery.

I don't get fouled up as often as I used to, and that's due in part to experience. I've been into the bush often enough to know the lay of the land in the north country. Faced with a different type of environment I'd likely keep map and compass clutched in my hot little hand. But I've come to know this territory well enough to feel at home in it and understand it.

Perhaps I've even developed a small reputation for being knowledgeable about portions of the area, because every so often some young person will show up with a trip plan and ask me to go over the route, explaining what I know about it. Aside from feeling flattered I also feel quite helpless. You see, the map doesn't show the dead pine I use as a landmark or the odd groups of rocks at the head of the better channel to follow. The map doesn't take into account the great change in water levels from spring to fall, and the map doesn't show the alternate portages I know of for some locations when, for example, spring flooding makes the summer portage useless.

The young person asks me questions, and my inner tape runs as I mentally paddle the route, spotting features and marks, noting small details that are stamped on my mind. When I look at the maps at such times, it's as if I'm delivered back to that place, and part of me sees and hears and feels all the special things that are intimately a part of a wilderness canoe trip. I feel the sense of peace one finds when leaving a windy, open lake and heading into a quiet, narrow bay where a seldom used portage waits. I hear the white-throated sparrow call from shore. I blink as a pair of dragonflies dart in front of my face. I blink, and I see only the map, my finger tracing the route I once followed. My mind recalls a host of details, such as the thick stand of reeds where red-wing blackbirds form a noisy, colored flurry of activity. Part of me feels sad because I'm not there. Another part of me knows there is no way I can convey to my young guest the full beauty of what the map vaguely represents. But before I'm done I hope to communicate a sense of what's out there, knowing that the very best of it, that which I can't put into words, will be there for others to discover just as it was for me.

Knots and Lashings

Work and life in the outdoors is aided by some knowledge of knots. As you are more than likely aware, there are books and books on knots and lashings. It is fascinating and detailed work, some of it. However, the basic knots used in camping are not complicated, and they are listed as follows:

Square Knot. Useful in bandaging and tying up packed items.

Fisherman's Knot. Used to join two ropes of the same size where strength is needed.

Sheet Bend. Used to join a smaller rope to a larger one.

Half Hitches. Used to attach cord to trees or for painter ropes, etc.

Tautline Hitch. Used for guy ropes because tension can be adjusted.

Bowline. A simple rescue knot that will not slip.

Timber Hitch. Used to bind to a tree or log where sideways pull would distort another hitch or cause it to slip.

Clove Hitch. Used most often in lashings.

Slippery Knots. These are made by tucking the free end of the rope back into the knot. When the end is pulled the knot will come apart quickly.

As I mentioned, there are plenty of books on knots. The most common source is the Scout Handbook or Scout Fieldbook. Those do a good job of showing knots and lashings, and they are readily available. In a few instances you may find the more elaborate books a bit hard to figure out. However, most knot work you'll need is pretty obvious. My list gives all standard, common knots, but the Fisherman's Knot was called the Water Knot at one time.

Simple camp lashings can be done with cord. Square and Sheer lashings are most common, but from time to time a Tripod lashing is used. Camp lashing is less fussy than the structural or engineering lashing taught in the better books. Two or three wraps around the wood followed by three or four fraps will secure most temporary structures.

I've had good results constructing large sheers for use with the rain tarp in heavy winds. One leg of the sheer points into the wind, and this prevents the tarp from forming such a large pocket.

In a matter of a few minutes a simple table for holding pots and pans can be lashed between two trees. If the trees are small the pots will simply rest between the two rails, even if they are not flat. However, a better surface can be made using bark, or even a web of ropework. Such a temporary table gets things off the ground, and it doesn't harm the trees.

Once you become familiar with knots and lashings you'll find they creep into your camp. If you move camp frequently, well, there is less time for such things. But when you stay put for a day or two or are faced with rough weather, lashings and knots can help to provide a more comfortable camp.

Fix Up Your Food

Good, tasty, appealing, attractive meals — who could argue with that? Today's prepared trail foods are quite good; they certainly surpass the days when campers were told to SOAK-SOAK-SOAK their meals (four hours of soaking was recommended as a minimum, overnight soaking when possible). Not very convenient, those early trail foods, and the taste, well, even after all the soaking you could give them the taste was a lot like simmered sawdust. Those first products for campers inspired me to try to improve my trail meals long ago.

It's become my habit to experiment with trail foods. A favorite variation is to use additional condiments. Curry or chili sauces for rice dishes, herb seasonings for fish, concentrates of onion or garlic, grocery store mixes for salad dressings or gravy can be used to liven up otherwise bland trail meals. Makers of trail foods tend to favor meals with large, average appeal, and that can make for dull eating.

Makers of trail foods also have various side dishes, such as vegetables, mushrooms, etc. and these can easily be added to existing meals. Quite often I've found some trial packs are improved greatly by including a packet or two of quick-cooking soup mix. And a meal can be given more bulk by adding instant rice or instant potatoes, in chopped or mashed form. Starting with a trail meal as a base, you can customize your meal. Between the camping store and grocery store, you have *many* options.

A technique I've found for beefing up meals on canoe trips in the North is to increase desserts. This does two things: One, it helps meals last longer, providing useful activity for long summer evenings. Two, substantial desserts add energy needed by active, outdoor people.

Using an aluminum dutch oven for baking, one can easily do cakes, brownies, rolls, sweet or plain bread, and cobblers. Trail food fruits, fruit sauces, or instant puddings go well with baked goods as toppings or sides. Some trail food desserts require no baking, but those that are actually baked are superior in quality and appeal. Baking mixes found in the grocery store are easily adapted to the trail; many require only adding water, mixing, and baking. An old standby for use in the bush is Bisquick, which can be used in countless ways. More complex mixes found in the grocery store can be used, too, by adding powdered milk, (use twice the amount of powder called for to make a given amount of liquid), liquid margarine, or dehydrated egg. To be sure, I experiment with the trickier mixes at home by preparing the mix with substitute ingredients as I'd do in the bush, and then baking in my home oven.

Fine tuning and experimenting with meals is a pre-camping activity which you'll improvise to suit your tastes and interests. Not so, however, the basic categories of trail foods open to you. Following are the major choices:

Raw or uncooked fresh foods. These make tasty meals and are preferred by some campers, especially for the first day or two. On extended trips, however, it becomes difficult to keep things fresh or unsmashed. In addition, fresh foods weigh more because they have all their water, and they require more preparation and cooking time. Results with fresh foods can be excellent, and the costs are often favorable, but weight and perishability make them an option I seldom use.

Retort pouch foods. A retort pouch is, essentially, a freshly cooked meal sealed in a plastic/foil pouch, instead of a can. A retort pouch looks odd at first, but it turns out to be an excellent way to capture food quality, far better than what comes out of a can. A retort pouch is "cooked" by dropping it into boiling water for five minutes or so—then it's done and ready to eat. Quality is good, but these meals weigh a lot. If I insisted on having fresh food for my first night, these would be a fine choice as they are fresh in taste, yet cook quickly—a real advantage when I'm running late, as always seems to happen the first day out. Such convenience and quality has a cost, though, making this an expensive way to feed a group.

The categories below are my "staples" for canoe trips. I use foods from both categories and will explain why.

Dehydrated trail food and dehydrated grocery store food. Prepared meals coming in this fashion contain no water and require at least 20 minutes of cooking time. These meals are light in weight and will keep well.

Their sealed container packets are well suited to packing and trail use. The cost per person is below that of retort pouches, but above that of fresh food. In general, dehydrated foods are a practical and affordable choice.

These meals, because of their longer cooking times, are appropriate for use on long summer evenings when a more instant meal leaves the camper with too little to do. When cooking dehydrated meals, people gather near the fire where they wait and socialize; the entire process provides more activity than simply wolfing down a quick meal. I've come to look forward to these longer meal times as an important part of the camping experience.

While dehydrated meals are often gruel or stewlike concoctions that become boring after a while, there is one dehydrated product I prefer over its higher priced competition. That is eggs. Dehydrated egg takes some practice to learn how to cook, and it benefits greatly by flavoring from cooked sausage (I make frequent use of smoked salami or summer sausage to go with eggs or pancakes. A lightly browned circle of sausage becomes the center of a bullseye pancake when batter is poured directly over the sausage.) or the addition of liquid margarine, grated cheese, etc.

Freeze-dried foods. These are the top-of-the-line in convenience, light weight, and quality (especially the major, evening meals). But each portion will cost two or three times what a portion of dehydrated food will run. This large difference in cost covers the prime advantages of freeze-dried products, which are (1) high quality foods that (2) cook in five minutes—a real blessing in nasty weather. In using freeze-dried meals it is necessary to go *long* on portions. For big-appetite teens, I use a four-person pack for two. I commonly plan on feeding only three people from a four-person pack.

Now here's how I use freeze-dried and dehydrated foods in my meal plan. A six-day trip requires five evening meals. In times when the weather is apt to be decent, I'll pack three dehydrated and two freeze-dried evening meals. During times when bad weather is more likely, I switch that ratio. Then, during the week, I use the following strategy: If we're running late and are really hungry and tired the first night, I'll use a freeze-dried meal as a convenience. After that, freeze-dried meals are to be used either *last* or when it *rains*.

In a light rain, I'll spend time cooking a dehydrated meal—we don't have much else to do, anyway. And of course, when the weather is fine and we're on schedule, the half hour or so that goes into preparing a dehydrated meal is of no consequence.

But there are times in the bush when the weather is blowing up a storm. Even if you had a good fire going, the wind and rain will chill it enough to make cooking difficult or even impossible. A large pan will prevent some rain from quenching the fire, as will an overhang from your rain tarp, but a steady downpour will cause most fires to barely stay alive, leaving little heat for cooking. Trying to cook a dehydrated meal under those conditions is a sad affair, and you'd better be ready to spend lots of time to achieve a barely passable result.

When it turns nasty, that's the time to bring out your camp stove and a freeze-dried meal that will cook in five minutes. I carry a Coleman Peak One stove, (I used to use the Coleman Sportster, but the Peak is much hotter and faster) and use it to boil up the water needed to feed my group. The camp stove will heat the water in short order, and we're soon ready to add the freeze-dried meal, which will reconstitute without further cooking. This can all be done conveniently under the rain tarp, and a cold, tired group of people doesn't have to endure the agony of a long-delayed meal because of the weather.

Freeze-dried foods and the camp stove are a blessing on days with foul weather or awful schedules. So, aside from reflecting your tastes, your menu plan should include a way to cope with harsh weather. Good teamwork, experience, and consistent methodology would allow you to cook dehydrated or raw foods during some pretty nasty conditions. It can be done. I can brag about having done so often enough in the past. But I don't miss the days when we ate soggy, cool food that was half-cooked over fires that produced masses of eye-burning smoke and little heat. I'd trade those days for a freeze-dried meal and a camp stove anytime.

Two North Woods Recipes

Few things represent the cultural, traditional flavor of the north woods more than Ojibway Fry Bread. I had my introduction to this delicacy when the ladies of the Grand Portage Reserve prepared a welcoming meal for the school faculty. The rich wild rice dish mixed with mushrooms and fried pork was excellent, but the hot, freshly made fry bread was even better. As far as I'm concerned, nobody does fry bread better than the people of Grand Portage. Here is their recipe:

Ojibway Fry Bread

(4–5 servings)

Into a bowl, pour:

2 cups flour. Form a well or pocket in the flour.

Adding the water last, into the well, put:

1 tablespoon baking powder
1 pinch salt
1 teaspoon sugar
¼ teaspoon yeast
1 cup warm water

Allow the water to bubble with the baking powder for a moment before stirring slowly and *very* thoroughly, pulling all ingredients together. After mixing, cover and allow to sit for a half hour.

I've heard of native families who, fifty years ago, would mix a batch of fry bread every afternoon and let it rise in a covered kettle on the canoe bottom until they made camp and fried it that evening. The dough is not as delicate as some cake or bread doughs, which can't take much rough treatment.

In a fry pan, melt:

½ pound of shortening

Your shortening should be about ½-inch deep, and it should be hot, but not smoking, because you want to fry and brown the bread and not scorch it.

Each fry bread piece is pulled away from the dough in a lump about the size of a rounded tablespoon. It's better if the lump is a bit elongated rather than rounded, so don't be afraid to stretch the dough. Each piece goes into the hot grease where it will brown and then be turned. Over a wood fire, keeping track of the progress of three pieces of fry bread in a pan at a time is plenty. As you remove one it is replaced by another, and so on. They need to cool some before you can eat them, but they are best when eaten warm. Some people dress them up by sprinkling them with a mixture of cinnamon and sugar, but I like them plain.

If I make fry bread twice during the week I'll plan on using altogether a full pound of shortening for the two frying sessions. The second time is always better because a little of the fry bread taste trapped in the remainder of the first half of the shortening gives the second batch more flavor. At home you can save your fry bread grease more easily. Batches from used grease are the best, so long as your grease isn't too old or burned.

The next north woods delicacy is fish. Most of our fish don't taste at all fishy, because our lakes are clear, cold, and very clean. But some people still object to the idea of fish. Set down a beautiful and lean herring fillet that's been battered and deep fried, and they wrinkle their noses and fuss, as if you were foisting on them a tawdry fish stick with freezer taste. These are the people who try to kill the taste of fish by covering the flesh with tartar sauce. For them I offer one of the smoothest recipes for fish they will ever have the pleasure of trying.

North Woods Fish

Into two quarts of water add:
    ¼ cup vinegar
    ½ medium onion, sliced into strips
    2 to 4 bay leaves
Heat this mixture in preparation for your fish, which you can be cleaning while the broth heats. This broth can cook slowly for as long as forty-five minutes before adding the fish.

Your fish should be in big chunks, as opposed to fillets. Pieces as wide as the average hand are appropriate servings, and it's best if the pot is fairly full of fish, so the pieces don't move around and fall apart while cooking. Simmer your fish and broth for twenty minutes, and it's done. Served with a hot noodle dish, it's excellent and nutritious.

I've used all sorts of fish with this recipe. It works very well with trout, walleye, and smallmouth. If you don't mind taking the time to constantly pick bones, it's very good with northern pike. You could, of course, boil fillets and thus avoid most of the bones, but when boiling fish most fillets will fall completely apart, whereas big chunks with the bones still in will stay intact.

Fold Up Your Tent

It gets abused by storage in a damp basement, or ignored in the baking confines of attic or car trunk. Tents often take more punishment at home than they get in the bush. We can't eliminate all hazards, but we can think about our portable shelter and give it better treatment, starting with how it gets folded.

When you're out camping and will set up the same tent later in the day, a bit of residual moisture or dew won't cause much trouble, aside from adding weight. Some water can be shaken from the fly, but often one has to fold a dampish or wet tent. This is not serious unless you keep a wet tent packed for days, especially if it's warm. An hour or two of sun and breeze when the tent is set up in the afternoon or evening will dry the interior. A cozy sleeping space is achieved more quickly if you open up the storm flaps fully, closing them before the damp of evening creeps in.

To fold or set up, I prefer using two people, one to work each end of the peak. In the following description, we'll deal with taking down and folding a tent such as the Eureka 4-person Timberline.

Start by releasing the fly at its corner, side, and shock cord connections. The fly ridge is then released, and both workers lift the fly at its center while moving the entire fly to one side of the tent. Lifted and dragged off in that fashion, the fly is folded in half and ready to "drop," center rib up, alongside, but clear of, the still standing tent.

With the fly off, you can see that the top of the rear vent and door panel have been left open six to eight inches, which allows air to escape after the tent is free of its frame. On a Timberline, you release the top shock cord loop and side clips, allowing the tent to fall and begin deflating. Incidently, complete deflation takes longer under damp, humid conditions.

While the self-supporting A-frame is being removed, the floor of the tent remains staked—a real convenience when it's windy, because the tent will flatten out better without the wind tumbling it. Bag the frame after disassembly, being careful not to drop poles into the bag, a sure way to punch holes in the pole bag. Double-check to see you've got all your poles (the best way is to count), and stack the connection or junction pieces over one pole in order to avoid the bulge created by junction pieces placed side-by-side. The filled pole bag, roughly one-third the tent width, is placed near the rear of the tent.

When the tent is flat and deflated, square it up by tugging the material into straight lines, pretty much following seam and floor lines to do so. I usually flip both A-shaped panels so their peaks are in the center, and while doing so I try to spread the excess material evenly. It doesn't have to be perfectly neat; a reasonably smooth distribution of material is fine. Between you and your partner, you'll soon have a neat-looking rectangle of material.

Now the fly is returned to the tent. It is lying alongside, center rib up, so all you have to do is take it by the center and drag it over the tent until the fly covers the rectangle. The fly stays folded in half, so it's merely a matter of laying the fly over the tent. It may be necessary to even the fabric a little or toss in corners if they stick out.

The last four stakes are now ready to be removed and put in their bag. (It's a good idea to count them, too.) Unstaked, the tent is more vulnerable to the wind, and a good gust can scramble your work. While folding, it helps if *folded* rather than *open* edges face the wind. Open edges form a pocket, which the wind will balloon open. When I start folding, I take wind direction into account. The fly goes on the *downwind* side of the tent, so when it's laced back over the tent, the *folded center* faces into the breeze.

Neatly squared up and covered with the halved fly, the tent is now ready to be folded into thirds. With one person on each end, this goes quickly. Make your first fold into the wind. The second fold will cover the open edge, protecting it from the wind, but you may still have to hang onto the fabric to keep the breeze from tossing it.

The tent is now a long strip of material, one-third as wide as it was before. The tent was set up over a plastic ground cloth, carefully folded back to be at least six inches smaller than the tent floor in all directions. The ground cloth keeps the tent floor cleaner and drier, while also providing a decent area on which to work. Some people think a ground cloth is useless extra weight, but they get to kneel in the mud when their tent is rolled, which is what happens next.

(First, though, a brief word about the ground cloth. After your tent is rolled, the ground cloth is shaken and folded. With two people, it's almost like folding sheets. The folded ground cloth should end up as an approximate twenty-inch square that's less than an inch thick. These folded squares make good padding for the backs of equipment packs, and they help shape packs, too.)

Now to roll the tent. The pole bag was at the rear of the tent, and it is now placed on the tent where the fabric will be rolled around it, giving the roll inner support and keeping the poles safely tucked out of harm's way. Roll slowly, as some trapped air must still escape at seams, etc. Forcing air out will disturb your roll and can place bursting pressure on seams. Fully rolled, the tent is tied round the middle with a short cord to prevent unrolling. (Left untied, a tent in a pack soon becomes a sloppy, saggy mess that won't stay put.) The rolled and tied tent goes into its sack or carry case, which provides a bit more protection for the material. If you have a number of similar tents, ID marks can be placed on the sacks, saving some confusion over which tent is used by which campers.

I roll my tents from back to front, so I always know which end is which, even when rolled. This practice speeds set-up because you know where the door will be without having to open the tent to find it. Doing it the same way all the time also makes it possible for someone else to set up my tent quickly, in the event that a fast-approaching storm requires that tents be set up while I'm doing something else. Use of the ground cloth speeds set-up where your tent has to fit between standing trees. In that situation, if the ground cloth will fit in the space available, you know the tent will, too, and it's easier to try different positions using the ground cloth alone rather than the entire tent.

If you are in the habit of *not* zipping up the door and screen (except for top vents) panels when you fold and roll, you stand a good chance of over-stretching the front opening when the tent is staked. A stretched front places tremendous strain on the zippers, the only door seal you have. A number of times I've seen people ruin zippers on their tents by trying to zip the door shut *after* pitching the tent tight. If you keep the door zipped across the bottom and most of the side, then you can't distort the front as easily.

On uneven ground, I'll pitch a tent a little sloppy or saggy rather than strain it. On some slopes it's almost impossible to get a good pitch. It's most important to avoid stretching your tent over a hollow or depression. Then, when you enter, be careful with your boots. People kneeling in a tent are unaware of how much force goes into the tips of their boots and, therefore, into the tent floor. Boot tips cause stretch pockets that weaken your floor, the same floor that helps keep you dry. Climbing boots with hard, crisp toes are deadly in that respect. Avoid letting your boot toes dig into the fabric.

When operating zippers I often use both hands, one to tug the zip tab gently, the other to guide the fabric or hold the zipper in line. Over the years, I've developed a *feel* for using zippers, and my fingers tell me promptly if there's a grass stem, pine needle, or bit of sticky sap in the teeth. I can't give you that *feel*, but I can assure you that it can't be felt if you move too fast. Most zippers are damaged by hasty, forceful action that insists on going forward when the situation calls for patient backtracking. Treating your zippers in cavalier fashion can lead to long nights as you try to sleep midst the hummm of the world's happiest mosquitoes – the ones trapped inside your tent.

What I have described here is most appropriate for groups on a canoe trip. In backpacking, for example, it's more practical to divide up portions of the tent rather than keep it in one bundle. But for canoe trips, I've found the procedure detailed here to be effective. For most parties of eight people, I'll have four tents. Three tents ride in a specialty pack I had made just for that purpose. The fourth tent goes on one side of an equipment pack. The tent pack with tent stakes, three Eureka Timberlines, three ground cloths, and maybe a few pack rods or other gear is one of the heaviest packs in the kit. But as each tent weighs approximately ten pounds, the total weight of the pack creeps somewhat over forty pounds, well within reason.

At home, erect your tent and dry it *completely*. But if you set up a tent on the lawn in hot sun, it is sure to draw in moisture from below. If necessary, hang it on a clothesline, place cardboard under it, or set it up on a dry concrete or wood floor. The lowest seams and shock cords will be the last to dry, so check them. Make sure, too, that the frame is empty of all water, as shock-corded frames will hold moisture and release it later into your tent, causing mildew stains or white, powdery aluminum oxides to form on your nylon. Your completely dry, folded, and rolled tent, in its storge or packing case, is best stored in a dry environment that doesn't get too hot. Being tightly rolled or frozen does not seem to have any impact on the nylon, but excessive heat will take some life from the fabric.

Tent Door

In *The Spirit of Canoe Camping* I recommended a tent door and screen that zipped across the bottom and one side. Since that time, I've had some queries about that recommendation. Is it some bias or prejudice on my part? Lots of tents come with doors and screens that zip down both sides. Why don't I like that newer design?

There is a reason. If you'll reflect on it you will soon imagine what a door that zips down both sides would be like. In order to get in or out, the door and screen must be unzipped fully. In a driving rain, that opens the interior of the tent too much, and it allows the door and screen to get into the dirty splash area low on the tent. Not only does the material get dirty, but it has a chance to pick up debris that can clog the zipper.

Of course, you could carefully place the door and screen inside. A little extra water would come in that way, though. The extra caution required would leave the interior more exposed to the weather for a longer period. The process of having to go over the door and screen is trickier than going through a door and screen that remain hanging, even partially.

Someone suggested to me that you only had to unzip one side and squeeze through the opening. That procedure may work for slim teens who camp in the nude. A full-bodied person wearing clothes will find that things like buttons will catch in the opening. There is also a fair amount of stress put on the fabric.

However, aside from wet weather, there is a reason why I dislike the door and screen that unzips down both sides. The reason is the common mosquito.

You may have noticed that mosquitoes are attracted to heat. They will hover close to the upper part of the body. By a tent, the greater numbers of them will swarm around the upper part. A door and screen that opens from the top down simply allows the greatest number of mosquitoes to join you in the tent. Slipping quickly inside is the desired goal, and it can hardly be done with that door design.

My preference for the door and screen that unzips along the bottom and one side has a reason. This design allows a corner of the door to be opened so that one can slip in quickly. Unzipping about 2½ feet up and 2½ feet across gives a small opening that does not open the tent to much weather or many insects. You can duck inside in a hurry.

On buggy nights some teamwork will help. When you are both ready to retire, one of the pair kneels down and unzips the door opening. While that is being done, the other person uses a bandana to whisk mosquitoes away from the area. When the door is open, the person kneeling shoots through the opening and gets out of the way so that the other can follow. Once inside, the second person grabs the corner of the door and screen and holds it in place with one hand while closing the zippers with the other hand.

The combination of a small opening, quick entrance, insect whisking, and quick closure does keep the number of insects coming inside to a minimum. Some will get in, but they can be hunted down before you settle down to sleep. On a buggy night, you may still have a dozen or more mosquitoes inside, but it would be many times worse if you had the other style of door.

In Your Tent When It Rains

Being in a tent when it's raining is about as close as a person can get to a rainstorm without getting wet. Compared to the dry security of a house, a tent makes you feel vulnerable. You are, after all, just one thin layer away from the out-of-doors, so you feel, hear, and even smell each new wave of the storm as it rumbles by. A violent storm will worry or frighten you, it's almost unavoidable. Lightning flashes that flicker through the fabric layers are not very comforting, and feeling the ground shake from the thunder isn't likely to put you at ease, either.

It is rare, however, that a person is actually injured while tenting in a storm. It can happen, but it's not common. Lightning may be the most frightening element, but it's probably the wind that will produce more injuries. So, try to avoid placing tents near or under trees with large dead branches that might get ripped loose in the wind. In a tornado-like storm there is almost nothing you can do to protect yourself, because even healthy trees will topple over and there is simply no way to know exactly how a storm will hit until it's already done so. I've sat through some pretty rough weather though, and I've yet to see any serious damage.

Most of the time you'll find a storm almost comforting as it drums on the tent fabric and beats rhythms on the vegetation. Curtains of rain slatter on the tent roof, coming in cycles like prankish visitors. Once you get used to the idea of being "out" in a storm, it can be quite interesting to have a seat so close to one of nature's shows.

After one stormy night in your tent you'll know how the temperature change that accompanies a storm feels and how long it lasts. You'll know that the brunt of a storm usually comes right away, then the rest becomes quite steady until it fizzles out, the final drops falling not from the clouds but from the trees. It's an education in weather to spend a night on the ground with only a tent wall between you and wet misery.

Of course, the misery can come inside to get you, and it's not unheard of for a tent to leak. In a driving, gust-blown rain even the best tents will allow water to seep in at seams, and a heavy rain will actually cause a mist to form inside as cloudlike particles of moisture are forced through the woven fabric.

To outsmart the misery you have to make spot checks and keep yourself away from the sides and ends of the tent. A sleeping bag resting against an outside wall, even lightly, will pick up moisture. Or, if a leak wiggles its way inside, you at least want to stay out of its path. Look around the edges of your tent with your flashlight every hour or so during a heavy downpour. If you spot a trickle, head it off with your towel and keep an eye on it.

Still, if your tent is situated in a depression, your tent floor may become a pool; the same fabric that keeps water out will also hold it in, once it gets in. I try to camp on a level or slightly inclined spot, as opposed to one that forms a mini-valley. Having a plastic ground cloth under the tent is extremely beneficial in very wet conditions. A nylon tent floor is waterproof, but when that floor is pressed by your body weight onto soggy ground, well, it's going to get damp, at least. A plastic ground cloth provides positive protection against that. To be effective, your ground cloth *must not* stick out past the area of the tent floor. I fold my ground cloth back at least six inches on each side so the tent floor overlaps it in all directions. Because I'm careful about that, I can only recall two times when particularly vigorous trickles of water got past my defenses and formed puddles on my ground cloth.

Through experience, I've developed a small host of behaviors having to do with keeping the inside of a tent dry in the rain. For example, during the day, while I'm still carrying on outdoor activities, I try to stay out of the tent because each trip inside brings in some water. Things I might need from inside the tent are placed near the door so I can reach them without going in after them. When I do go in, I leave the wet raingear at the door, as opposed to bringing it across the tent, dripping all the way. The same holds true for wet boots and socks. Keep those things by the door, thus keeping the rest of the tent drier.

When settling down for the night I edge toward the center of the tent. I sleep without moving much during the night, but if my companion is one who moves I'll place the emptied personal pack between him and the outside wall, giving him a barrier that helps keep him from resting against the tent and getting damp. When it's rainy I tell myself to wake occasionally and check the tent, my partner's sleeping position, etc. In short, I'd rather force myself to wake for a few minutes at 2 a.m. and find a quarter pint of water forming a puddle near my sleeping bag than to sleep until 6 a.m. when I discover I have cold feet from two pints of water that have thoroughly soaked in.

If kept in plastic bags, the rest of your gear is safe from getting wet, but your sleeping bag is a big, exposed target. It will, at the very least, pick up quite a bit of humidity from the air. So, in damp weather the rule is this: Leave Your Sleeping Bag Exposed to Humid Air as Little as Possible. Laid out flat, it has more area to absorb humidity. Packed away and put inside its plastic bag for the day it won't get any drier, but it won't continue to absorb moisture from the air. In rainy weather your bag is the last thing to uncase and the first thing to put away.

Once you remember you're in a tent, close to the outdoors, where silly mistakes count against *your* comfort, then living in a tent becomes a simple, practical matter. You get so that you like it. Having to sleep inside a house suddenly feels rather confining and stuffy. It becomes second nature to keep the interior of the tent organized and orderly. (After all, how would you spot a tiny trickle of water if you scattered your clothes helter skelter all over the place?) You adapt yourself to basics, and you find that your behavior takes into account the conditions surrounding you. You pay keen attention to details, a trait quickly learned after you are careless once and allow a tent door to go improperly closed in the rain, thus forming a channel that directs a rivulet at your sleeping bag.

Some people, however, place their faith in better equipment. I've been told by outdoor enthusiasts that I wouldn't have to worry about getting wet in my tent *ever* if I just bought the "super tent" they proudly own or sell. Phooey! I don't believe it. Any nylon tent used on a regular basis can and will allow water inside. Resealing seams is necessary. Touching up portions of the fabric needing repellent is necessary. What the enthusiasts are really saying is that a new tent is more waterproof than a well-used one, but I already know that.

My point is that the tent user is the real quality control. A careless user will get wetter more often than a careful one. But no tent is going to be 100 percent perfect when faced with nature's surprises. I've been in weather so odd that I wasn't sure where the water was coming from. Once our camp was shrouded in soupy fog accompanied by two days of warm drizzle. Fabric couldn't breathe, so the condensation inside was about equal to the fog outside. In that situation the water gave us a sneak attack, but a direct frontal action will penetrate a tent, too, as you'll find out when you ride out a gale of rain.

Recently a devotee of a "better" tent described its merits to me in abundant detail. He was particuiarly glowing about the tent's fabric tubes, which held the frame in place. He was right in saying that fabric tubes do a good job, but I am familiar with the brand of tent he described because a client of mine insisted on using one on a canoe trip. The fabric tubes into which the poles must slip were, in my mind, a time-consuming nuisance. If you are in a hurry, the tubes are a real detraction. I can recall many times when I've raced a coming storm, gotten ashore, and started to pitch my tent minutes before the first drops hit. As soon as the tent is up and my personal gear safely inside, I want every extra moment for gathering and covering dry firewood.

So why should I take extra time to slip the tent frame into cloth tubes? No good reason I can think of. Now, I have to agree that a tent with pole tubes will hold its shape better in a wind. But what's the advantage in that? Put a tent with tubes alongside one with an exposed frame and keep increasing the wind. The same thing will happen to both of them: They will collapse when the wind load exceeds the strength of the frame. If you're in a wind that determined, you can bet that a few nylon pole tubes aren't going to matter much.

The strength of the frame is of more importance than whether or not the tent has pole tubes, and all modern tents have exactly the same vulnerability if they have a fly covering the tent. The fly is the vulnerable feature and it's very difficult to anchor one any better than the way most manufacturers have come up with. So, the fly is the weakest link. Yet for those times I've had my tents hammered by awesome winds that actually curled a few of them into balls, not one of my supposedly "inadequate, external-framed tents" ever had the fly torn off.

But I have been told how foolish I am to rely on old-fashioned external-frame tents. I've been told I really should have tents that come with strong guy lines to properly anchor them against heavy winds or gusts.

Sounds sensible, doesn't it? What could be wrong with having guy lines to secure your tent against the worst nature has to offer? Well, it's true the guy lines will save you from nature, but not from people. Yes, people. Just stop a minute and figure out what happens when a 150-pound teenager hits that guy line and pulls it down with him. All the stress and strain of such an accident goes into the small portion of the frame, which bends into a sharp kink. You'd have to go camping in tornados to do that in a wind, but it's simple if just one person lands heavily on your guy line.

No, friends, I'll stay with my Coleman A-Frame or my Eureka Timberline, each with its old-fashioned exposed frame. I can put one up in the dark and never fumble once. I can put one up before that better tent is even half up, and I don't have to hurry to do so. And if it gets windy I can attach guy lines and secure the tents as needed (Eureka added D-rings to the fly for that purpose years ago). It's very simple. I pack along one long clothesline of parachute cord for each tent, and if it gets real windy the clothesline becomes a tent guy. What could be less complicated than that? You see, if you can learn to use your head about such matters, you're on your way to becoming a better camper. *You* can do what the equipment can't, and that is to think. Once you start to do so you'll find you're no longer vulnerable to the camping salesperson's hype. You can walk away from the latest "super tent" with never a regret. And I can guarantee you'll walk away with more money left in your account, too.

Field Guides, and Field Work

People frequently ask me what outdoor or nature books I recommend. Books about nature, in some respects, replace the human guide, while in other respects such books supplement the human guide. There is, of course, room for both. Aside from providing information, an outdoor book allows one to "voyage" during the off season. As good as a book is, though, it can't get as specific about little details in a given area as a working guide can. To be useful to a larger number of people, a book has to be more broadly informative.

The following books are ones I've turned to many times for reliable, basic information and ideas.

Scout Handbook, also *Scout Fieldbook*. Both of these have good general information and lots of decent camping tips. The *Fieldbook* is more advanced. The Fifth Edition (*Handbook For Boys*) edited by Ted S. Pettit in the 1950s, is one of the better handbooks. It has good nature information, though the camping ideas are somewhat dated. If you go looking for these in used book stores, don't pass up the old Merit Badge books, some of which are practical and concise.

How to Stay Alive in the Woods, by Bradford Angier is an old favorite of mine. I wore out my original copy. It's particularly good about northern areas.

A Field Guide to the Birds, by Roger Tory Peterson. What more can I say? It's a classic.

A Field Guide to Animal Tracks, by Olaus J. Murie is one of the best! Murie had a superb eye for detail. He combined art and science to make a truly useful book.

Excellent guides of a more regional character or guides to a specific park are available, too. For the Boundary Waters and Quetico area, I'm fond of *Plants Of The Quetico, Minnesota Rocks And Waters*, and Rutstrum's *North American Canoe Country*. But, there are many more good books, and some areas have been well blessed with dedicated researchers and writers.

Quite often I've read a book, tried some of its suggestions, then gone back to read again. In this way, I can modify what the book recommends against my experience and local conditions. In time, a person learns to adapt ideas, even though most of the basics aren't open to much change. The primary focus of nearly all outdoor books is either toward adventure-camping or nature. A good camping book helps us establish a goal or new ideal. A good nature book reminds us of nature's complexity and living beauty and both topics are worthy ones.

But be warned! Even in our best efforts we are biased, sometimes in tragic ways. For example, the plight of some creatures (such as doe-eyed fawns) gets more coverage than the fate of other animals in the wild. We are selective about what we support and believe. I don't know of a good, comprehensive book on insects. It's not a popular topic, so decent information in other than a college text format isn't available. The same is true of other topics, even with things like geology. A few subjects get most of the popular attention.

You may have guessed that I'm building up to something, and I am. I want to put in a few words for one of those topics that often gets skipped over.

Cultural or heritage resources cover a range from prehistoric to historic finds. Unlike a noble herd of caribou, heritage resources don't move to attract our attention. But, like caribou, once the habitat (in this case a site) is destroyed, it's gone for good. Natural erosion accounts for some site destruction, other sites fall prey to development, while many others are simply not recognized and are slowly erased. The point is simple, sites are easily ignored and easily destroyed, because the general public cannot distinguish a prehistoric site from a picnic site.

In the north, sites are often thin, maybe a few centimeters in depth. In addition, most visitors will not recognize anything but the larger, more obvious artifacts. Would you recognize a stone drill, thumbnail scraper, or siltstone adze? Such items can easily go unnoticed. The subtler aspects of archaeological sites stand even less chance — it takes training and the right methodology to recognize a soil feature, which is a faint stain in the ground indicating disturbance or intrusion. Today's campers spend time on prehistoric and historic sites without knowing it, and their activities help destroy those sites. What can be done.?

Joining a historic or archaeological society is a step, if you've a strong enough interest and wish to further develop it through training and programs. Through such groups you can support additional research; such citizen contributions are vital.

However, if you're like most people, your interest in the past will be strong, but not so strong that you'll want to join another organization because of it. That is, until you're out camping and you find something unusual. Then you'll want to learn more about it—a seemingly simple task, but one that can become quite tricky.

First, all finds should be reported. Depending on your area, the following represent the most logical places to begin reporting a site or to ask for information about sites and finds and how to report them:

State or provincial historical or archaeological societies
State or provincial college/university
Federal land management units (forest service, bureau of land management, park service all have access to archaeological services)

Making a report does not mean you have to surrender your find. It simply allows an agency or researcher to record the find and its location. If you find something, be as accurate about the location as possible. It's best if you draw a simple sketch giving elevation above water, distance from road, or whatever will help pinpoint the spot. In this way, information is gathered that might otherwise be lost, and it could turn out that your find is unusual, even important. I know one collector who was wont to show off his "good" stuff, which was mostly typical woodland arrowheads. An archaeologist once asked if he had any "junk" that he wasn't showing. At that, he produced several coffee cans of broken tools and other odds and ends. In one of them was a piece of pottery that was junk to him, but not to the archaeologist, who was amazed to learn that southern pottery had come this far north. Reporting your find means just that, reporting. They'll want to look at it, perhaps photograph it, but they won't confiscate it. And it could be that your report will be the only information for an area. Important sites don't get found if people like you don't make routine reports, so please share the information.

Sometimes professional archaeologists aren't very interested in what amateurs have to show or offer. Don't let the attitude deter you. You've just got to work past it; after all, the archaeologist probably gets more than his share of crackpots walking in off the street with proof positive that the Egyptians were in Minnesota. Or you may inadvertently bring a prehistoric find to a facility with a historic specialty, and they will be largely unable to record information from what you have or tell you much about it. But if you persist, you will eventually discover the appropriate agency charged with recording or protecting sites and able to tell you more about what you've found.

Having just encouraged the amateur archaeologists out there, I must now deliver an admonition. Many sites are routinely plundered by bottle collectors, pot hunters, curio seekers, and wreck divers. Those hobbyists are destroying information at an appalling rate. They are also, in many cases, breaking the law by digging into sites or in other ways disturbing them or removing things from them. A serious amateur *never* disturbs a site. The responsible amateur gathers evidence by keen observation of the surface forms and by what is found on an already disturbed surface. Excavations (even tiny ones) are work for trained professionals who will gather much useful information from a complete and methodical dig. Restrict your activity to examining surface finds only.

Four-Wheel Drive

When a person lives in a remote area that sees lots of snow in winter, the idea of four-wheel drive is appealing. I didn't need much of an excuse at all to arouse my interest; it just blossomed at the first opportunity. I had some good and practical reasons, of course, but going in search of my first four wheeler was more courtship than practical business.

I was seventeen at the time, and I had just come back with a little cash in hand after spending a summer working at Camp Wichingen. On the way back home I spotted a jeep with a "For Sale" sign on it.

The next day I was back to take a look. It was a 1952 military jeep, an M-38. It had a military hardtop with foam insulation, military tires, and two 12-volt batteries. There was an arctic gasoline heater, full radio plugs, deep water fording, and other miscellaneous options. It was a mechanical marvel. The owner said he had the military book on it, but he wasn't sure where it had gone to. I said, "As soon as you find the book, I'll buy it." I dug out my wallet with all that nice new money in it. He found the book.

I drove it home the same day while a friend followed. I was three hundred dollars poorer, but I felt on top of the world. Apart from a few rattles and jolts, I was purring down the road in my own four-wheel drive. That drive home alerted me to a problem with the directional signal the previous owner had installed — it didn't work. So, there were a few things that would have to be fixed.

All in all, I worked on that machine on and off for two years. The engine, a little four banger, had to be rebuilt. Wheel bearings and seals had to be redone. Body repairs had to be made. New tires were called for and a new paint job was needed, too. In two years there wasn't much I didn't pull off that machine and work on. Was it a good education? You bet!

That little jeep was just the right size for my age and ability. I used to read the military manual with the avidity formerly reserved for Playboy. I was absolutely amazed at the way the military planners had thought of everything. It took ten minutes to take off a single plug wire, but the darn things would never leak, short out, or interfere with the radio. Those plug wires looked more like garden hoses running from the sealed distributor to a plug.

Not only was I learning mechanics, but I had to take into account the military planning that went into the machine. I had to think in new directions and with a different frame of reference. The guys who made the M-38 may have long been retired, but the vehicle lived on long enough to teach me a few lessons.

When I wasn't working on it, I was driving it. Top speed was 45 mph. It would turn in its own shadow, or so it seemed. I had lots of fun with that machine. In my town, a boy with a jeep was not really desirable, but on a few occasions I did manage to park in the less observed areas of town. There was some reward, but once I got into a serious spot, the girls usually remembered duties calling back at home. In those days the chase was everything.

By the time I started college, which was three hundred miles away, I had determined that the jeep was no good on the highway. Cars screamed by at 65 and 70 mph. I was outclassed. So, the jeep stayed home and I took the train most of the time. I'd get back home once a month, and even in the coldest part of winter the jeep, with its 24-volt starting, would crank over and go.

I hated to give it up, but I didn't see how I could use it for road travel. It was too slow. In two-wheel drive, that high-bodied beast was treacherous on slippery roads; it loved to spin. In the summer it was so hot inside that I put an oak block on the gas pedal so my foot wouldn't burn up. It was fine for puttering around a rural area.

A few old-timers told me not to put a bigger engine in it. I didn't want to hear that, but they said a V-8 was just too much for a jeep designed for a four banger. I had to agree that if the military planners had thought a V-8 was the answer, the jeep would have had one. They hadn't missed a shot. So, I gave up on that idea and started to look around for a replacement.

Sometimes things work out with awesome swiftness. I had just made up my mind to replace the jeep when I found out about Land Rover. Northern Minnesota is an unlikely place for a Land Rover dealer, but when something is meant to happen it does. The world has always been marvelously strange that way.

The Rover people had a machine about the size of the jeep. It had a four banger, too, but they had added a fourth speed, whereas the jeep only had three. Rover claimed 55 to 60 mph for a road speed. It was slow for those days, but it sounded much better than the jeep. I found a Land Rover dealer in Hibbing on the Iron Range. In the frozen wastes of the north, there sat those machines, looking like they came out of an African safari movie. I was hooked.

It's one thing to afford a worn-out jeep. A new machine is a whole different story. The dealer had his first demonstrator, which was a year old, and he said he'd sell it for $1,500 less than its original price. That meant I needed $3,000 for the Land Rover. I got $750 for my old jeep, which was now quite nice and a good runner; the rest was borrowed.

It took a few weeks to get the whole deal tied up, but in the end I drove home with a Land Rover. What a machine. It looked exotic. I quickly fell to work on it, to fix it up with some extra goodies. Fog lights, rear wiper, radio, marker lights, spot, chain carriers, tool carrier, all got added over the next few years.

And I set about learning more about four-wheel drive. The Rover people had some large and expensive technical manuals. I bought them and began to learn how British engineers thought. There was even some new language involved—my favorite new word was *traficator*. It was a wonderful time.

The Rover was slow in comparison to other machines on the road. American companies were coming out with fast-travelling four-wheelers, and they all had V-8 engines. They'd scream by me on the road. But in tough going I could crawl and pull far more than the fast machines.

I learned why. The off-road machines, like my old jeep and the Rover, had a very high differential ratio. On the Rover it was 4.7 to 1. That's high. A ratio like that develops lots of traction and pull. It will leap off a starting line, too. But, it has no top speed. You can pile on more revolutions with a bigger engine, but it won't go much faster. It was designed to do certain things, and that is it. Period.

The other machines used bigger engines and lower differential ratios. They were primarily street machines with off-road capability. The Rover was an off-road machine with street capability. It was a nice distinction.

The Rover engineers even added a few specialized touches that forced the driver to actually drive. To begin with, they did not put syncromesh between first and second gear. You had to learn to double clutch in order to shift. More than anything else, that forced the driver to hear and feel his driving. It made you very aware of what was going on with the mechanical parts and pieces. You actually had to understand the machine in order to do well with it.

In an age of automatic transmissions most people thought I was daft to have such an old-fashioned arrangement. Maybe so, but having learned to drive a Rover, I've been able to drive anything less complicated with little adjustment on my part. After practicing the Rover engineer's instruction for doing multiple shifts through both transfer cases, I ended up with a feel for what was going on in those closed boxes full of gears.

I had driven that machine for more than eight years when I took it into a shop in Canada for main seal replacements. After the work was done, the mechanic asked if I did most of the driving. I told him, yes. He then told me that while the machine was apart, an inspector from the Rover Motor Company had come by. He had shown the inspector my clutch. "There's no wear on your clutch. It looks brand new. I guess if you drive these things the way they tell you to they just don't give out."

I was pleased. It had been simple enough to just follow the instructions — the Rover engineers knew their machine, and their directions were right on target.

I did buy another old-style four wheeler. It was a big military-type Dodge Power Wagon with two winches, enormous running gear, 900-X-16 tires, and a long body. It had the same characteristics as the Rover and jeep, and I used it for plowing snow. It ate snowplows. I never could make one strong enough to stand up to that truck. The pickup floor was solid, half-inch plate. It was like an animated mountain. It wasn't fast, but it would pull and work like nothing else I ever owned. When I got it, it had been badly abused, but the Dodge engineers had built a good truck, and it bounced back. It was a truly massive piece of work, and the front end spindle joints were a masterpiece.

So, I now recognize the engineering skill that goes into machines. It's there in foreign and American machines; it's just that there are different purposes in mind with some rigs. If they are driven sanely, they will do a fine job. Right now I'm using a Chevrolet ¾-ton pickup with two-wheel drive. It's eleven years old and there's 170,000 miles on the chassis. Pardon me if I don't look awfully serious when someone starts to talk about shoddy American products and engineering. It would take a lot to convince me.

No machine is perfect. Each one is set up to do certain things within certain limits. The manufacturers spell that out somewhere along the line. They do tell you what to do for optimal performance. And if you're wise enough, you can pick out power train and running gear options galore. They've got crossbreeds from straight off-road to straight street. The American firms produce four wheelers that make an old-fashioned heart go pit-a-pat.

The thing most often wrong with a four wheeler is the driver. Between impatience and excessive use of power, a bad driver can tear a machine apart, then complain that it wasn't built well. Poor drivers expect four-wheel drive to go anywhere. They want to show off, and they get into jams.

I've seen it happen often enough. They drive onto beach gravel and get bogged down. It's nearly flat on the beach, and they can't understand why they are stuck in just six inches of loose sand. Figure out the angle from the bottom of the tire to the place where it touches the sand in front. It's a lot like trying to drive up a cliff. They don't see the cliff because it's only six inches tall, but it is continuous. Every inch forward has to climb that cliff. And these people wonder why they get stuck.

They do the same thing in snow. Getting high-centered doesn't mean anything to them until it happens. Then they wonder why the manufacturer would build a vehicle that allowed all four wheels to spin uselessly just because the center of the vehicle rested on firmly packed snow.

They do it in mud. A good driver will get out and walk around an area to check it out. If it looks tough, then you figure a way around it, if possible. The ones with go-anywhere minds plow into it at a good rate of speed. If they're lucky, inertia carries them across. If not they consider buying a winch.

There is one law that operates here: The driver must do the thinking. Any machine can get bogged down, and if anything, a four wheeler will get more stuck in a more awkward place. That's the size of it, and if the driver just assumes four-wheel drive will take him anywhere his heart desires, well he's going to find out otherwise.

I like four-wheel drive. There are maybe six times each year when it really makes the difference. In a rural area, that's significant. There isn't much help around, and it beats being stranded for any length of time. If you're a real brush rat, then you've got two pair of tire chains, a winch, tow chains, snatch block, etc., as well as a shovel and other items for getting unstuck.

That's for when you *must* make some trek with the vehicle, despite the conditions. Otherwise, the sane thing is to pick the right time for going someplace. If you plan right, a tough go can be made a lot easier. Knowing your area as well as the capability of the machine means getting stuck a lot less often.

The simplest way to put it is this: After you get stuck, go back and read the book. It will tell you just what you should not have done. Next time, don't do it; then you won't get stuck. End of lesson.

II
A Guide's Stories

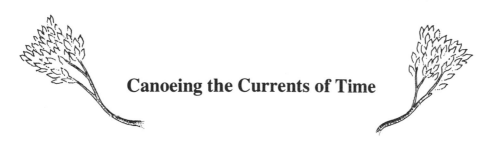

Canoeing the Currents of Time

After years of paddling 17- and 18-foot canoes, I was getting bored. No, bored isn't the right word to describe it, because I wasn't tired of canoeing. Quite the opposite, I wanted to do more of it or expand the experience further. In some ways, I'd done about all a person could reasonably do with a "traditional" canoe in a lakeland, paddle and portage wilderness. My inner mood was ready for a new twist on an old theme, and that's how my interest in big canoes was more than revived.

Like most others interested in this subject, my introduction to large canoes was through the fur trade. Large canoes are often called fur trade or voyageur canoes, as if such items were invented by European fur traders.

Fortunately, I was in a position to get over that delusion. My interest in prehistory and my access to excellent sources of information and research in Canada quickly began to fill in the prevoyageur picture. As my information grew it became more and more obvious that large canoes had been on the scene for a long time.

How long? Perhaps 10,000 years. Almost certainly 7,000 years. Back then Lake Superior was in various glacial phases, making it a much larger lake than it is today. On those ancient beach ridges, miles from today's shoreline, are sites used by prehistoric visitors and residents. It is a fairly good bet that peoples living alongside an inland sea would have developed (or were in the process of developing) substantial water transport. In a harsh climate, they had enough cultural technology to survive, and to do so they probably built shelters of bark or skin. The same basic technology (a pole framework covered by bark or skin) used in constructing shelters would have led to what we call the voyageur canoe. At that early date, the canoe may not have been fully developed, but 5,000 years ago there occurred a dramatic increase in artifacts related to fishing. Grooved stones were hung at the bottom of fishing nets, copper gaffs were used to snag big fish held in the nets — such artifacts strongly suggest a technology that included reliable, seaworthy vessels to facilitate the use of fish resources.

Even from an early period, then, there seems to have been a maritime tradition. I suspect, too, that once established, the tradition didn't change much, as peoples utilizing the area would have much the same needs and would follow similar methods for meeting them. It is likely that canoes in the 30- to 35-foot range were used from the Atlantic coast throughout the Great Lakes region — wherever there was "big" water. Inland of the Great Lakes there are large bodies of water, but certainly not demanding of the largest canoes. So, inland one would expect to find the use of 20- to 25-foot canoes for transport, and smaller canoes for specialty purposes. There may even have been some specialization among groups. For example, those adept at big-water fishing may have seldom been in a position to harvest wild rice in their large fishing canoes. Specialized groups, relying on differing technologies, may have traded goods and services as part of a large, overall survival scheme.

This is essentially the pattern of the fur trade, but I place it well prior to the start of the fur trade. If you are skeptical, you will probably ask what "simple" Indians needed with such big canoes when there were no imported trade goods to haul around. Well, I really don't think we Europeans invented trade, and there is a growing body of evidence that suggests such utilization of resources began immediately upon glacial melt. But even if we downplay trade, we must still admit that native peoples probably needed large transportation to move survival goods, preserved food, and family members, all on a seasonal basis. Unfortunately, little effort has gone into researching prehistoric technology and trade. Historic research covering the fur trade (our history) is much more popular with us than is the great unknown of prehistory (the history of other peoples). But we do know that fur traders could make a round trip from the Atlantic coast to the farthest point inland and return to the coast in one long summer season. There is no reason to believe that native peoples (at least some of them) were not doing the same thing earlier. After all, the European trader followed native routes that were well known and much used. If you are still doubtful, please think about the fact that no European trader had to teach native peoples how to trade or what trade was. They knew well what it was, and the Europeans were simply a new kind of trader to include in their seasonal survival rounds.

At this point, however, without further research it is simply educated speculation on my part to attempt to deduce what happened. I assume that large canoes were in frequent use, and while that is a guess, I believe it is a sound one.

Both academic curiosity and a desire to add to my canoeing experience led me to look for a 25-foot inland or north canoe to use in the canoe country north of the Great Lakes. It was not easy to find one. Our canoeing tradition south of the Canadian border is for small canoes used by two or three people. A *corporate* paddling tradition barely exists in the United States, so I looked in Canada, where 20- and 25-foot freight canoes are still used.

My source turned out to be the Wabasca Canoe Company in Wabasca, Alberta, a long way from my canoe country. By phone, letter, and with the help of drawings, I went over details with the builder. In particular I wanted low ends with small decks, forward rocker, seating for ten, a mast step, and a narrow bottom leading to straight or flared sides. Some of my wants were accommodated, others couldn't be, due to the nature of the building mold. For example, building over a mold meant a fixed tumblehome and rocker.

But the few compromises I had to make were more than compensated for by the quality of construction and the overpowering beauty of the result. Built of cedar with a canvas cover, the canoe was laid-up over a mold, which clenched the brass tacks used to secure strips to ribs. The color of fresh wood that's clear and sound is complemented by the obvious hand-fitting of ribs and the meticulous piecing of planks on the ends — all of which characterize a classic, hand-built canoe. It's like art that's made to be used, and over the years its patina will glow on the hull.

The real test, though, is to use and paddle the canoe. I soon found it would hold ten people and all their gear, but it was much more comfortable with nine and gear. When put down on paper, the logistics look awesome. Take nine people at 150 pounds each, add nine packs at 40 pounds each, add the weight of the canoe, paddles, lifejackets, and other miscellaneous gear, and you easily reach an average load that's close to 2,000 pounds. To a person accustomed to 17-foot tandem canoes, the idea of a ton of people and gear moving in one lump is difficult to accept.

The first time I loaded the canoe up with people and equipment, one of the passengers turned around and said, with concern, "How are we going to portage this thing?" Fortunately, it was a question I'd given much thought to. The 25-foot Wabasca weighs 235 pounds and carries nine people with ease. Using three standard canoes at 85 pounds each, you'd have 255 pounds of boat for the same nine people, slightly more than the weight of the big canoe. Of course, if most of the nine preferred tandem canoeing, you'd need four standard canoes, and would then have 340 pounds in boats, considerably more than the weight of the 25-footer. The use of lightweight tandem canoes shifts the numbers in favor of tandem canoes, but the weights remain roughly within 25 pounds of one another.

It's likely, though, that your mental lightbulb has lit up and you are thinking, "I'd rather move four, smaller loads than one, 25-foot killer. How do you manage to move such a chunk of weight?"

First of all, you don't use a canoe like this where portages are frequent or long. (By the same token, look at some of the big lakes in the Quetico/Boundary Waters area. You know that paddlers in small canoes avoid them as much as possible. So, a big canoe can put you in virgin territory right in the midst of canoe country and give you a greater choice of routes.) When you go to carry the big canoe, you do so in its floating or "up" position. Four adults can do it, one on each side of the bow thwart and one on each side of the stern thwart. The canoe is lifted less than a foot and walked forward. With four carriers, the average load per person is 58 pounds, less than most tandem canoes. It is a little awkward, but the big canoe can be toted across most portages separating the larger lakes.

If the weather is rainy, however, the cedar hull will absorb water and gain weight. The hull can easily pick up 60 or 80 pounds in additional weight—which is just as easily handled by adding two more carriers at the center thwart. If all nine people carry the canoe, the load per person is 26 pounds. At that rate, the canoe could absorb its own weight in water and the nine carriers would still only have to handle 52 pounds each. Within limits, portaging is no more of a problem with the big canoe than with any other.

But you are still wondering how it paddles. I've been saving that. It's best answered by stating, "Water is its element." Remember, you've got nine people paddling. Get a good pace going, and it's not difficult to do 10 mph. The paddling stroke is much like the racing stroke, a pull from forward to alongside, done in unison unless you want to see a tangle of paddles bashing together. When the crew really digs in, the canoe scampers, getting up to 15 mph or better for short bursts. But just think of moving twice as fast (at least) as you do in a tandem canoe, without having to exert yourself. Slightly more effort than you'd normally use in a tandem canoe will yield nearly three times more speed in the big canoe. Trips on big, long lakes are handled easily. During long summer days, think where eight hours of paddling would carry you at 8 or even 7 mph. A leisurely pace on a relaxed trip will still take you 30 or 40 miles per day with ease. Use of the 25-foot canoe cuts the area down in size and explains, in part, how prehistoric peoples could spread over a wide area by following huge glacial bodies of water with their craft.

Large canoes have another benefit, as well. They will not only tackle extensive daily mileage, they will do so on days that would keep a tandem canoe on shore. Once you get a ton of canoe, people, and gear moving, it takes quite a severe wind or rough water to turn it. It's an amazingly stable form of transport, especially to the paddler accustomed to fighting for progress together with one other paddler in a light canoe. My Wabasca canoe handled two-foot waves with ease, giving a secure and dry platform for paddling. Both mass and inertia contribute toward progress—once you get the canoe moving it will stay moving, without being nearly as affected by outside forces as a small canoe. We were able to travel on days when it would have been futile for two people in a 17 footer. And because the big canoe was seaworthy we were able to take straighter, quicker routes than you'd take with a small canoe. The capability of the larger craft was impressive, and having multiple paddlers gave sufficient power for the longest, windiest runs.

When I'd first begun planning for a 25-foot canoe, I assumed it would be hard to steer, requiring strong efforts on both bow and stern. Not so! Once under way, even the loaded canoe responds to a J-stroke just like a tandem canoe. To be sure, the stern steering stroke sometimes requires more effort, because there's more canoe to turn or adjust. But most of the time it is easy to paddle and steer, involving only moderate effort.

The hardest work with the canoe comes in getting it moving. The first few sweeps by the paddlers seem to do nothing. But once it starts to respond, it *responds*. Heaven help you if you are charging into shore too fast, for example. Similarly, any turns that have to begin from a standing start or at slow speed will require real effort. It's best to draw or pry the bow while doing the same at the stern, to pivot. Quick turns while underway also call for steering action from both ends in order to swing the canoe on its middle. And at times, a severe gust of wind may slew the bow more than stern corrections can handle, requiring the bow paddler to assist in steering. I feel more comfortable having an experienced paddler in the bow, but almost anyone can handle bow steering as long as they respond accurately to commands such as, "Bow. Switch sides and draw." or "Bow. Sweep, your side."

I've only one real regret about the 25 footer— I don't get to use it often enough. It's inconvenient to move around, and most canoeists are hesitant about trying something of the sort. But when I do find people who are willing to give it a try, we have safe and sociable trips on large lakes. Paddling together like that is a new kind of canoeing experience, and the craft does open up water that's avoided by smaller vessels. I've good memories of calm paddling with a happy group, and I've impressive recollections of the canoe handling rough going. A canoe such as my Wabasca comes with a long history, providing much more than transportation.

Camping Trip to Big Lake

Some stories should possibly never be told, and this one could qualify. But a glimpse of the nascent guide may be useful, and the situation itself may provide some amusement.

My guiding "instincts" got encouragement when I was a lad. That's how the trip to Big Lake came about. But it never would have happened at all if, a few years earlier, a local scoutmaster hadn't encouraged me to be a "leader." Being a "boy leader" meant doing lots of things the "adult leaders" didn't want to be bothered with. But I was young and felt more flattered than put upon. I was sixteen at the time, just entering a phase of heavy interest in backpacking. In my town I was the only one I knew of who thought the idea of walking long distances with a pack on his back was "fun." Kids my age had other interests—I needn't tell you what. It's enough to say that I had a devil of a time finding camping buddies. Luckily, that's where being a "leader" started to pay off.

It occurred to me that backpacking could be presented as a "reward" for some of the more capable Boy Scouts. Boys of fourteen were of an age to feel flattered when asked to go camping by an older outdoors lad, even though the invitation involved a long trek with a full pack. At that age, even if they saw my "trick" they might still agree to go along, because they'd not yet started the cycle of cars and girls. If I played my cards right I'd be assured a steady suppy of camping companions for years.

Nevertheless, the trip to Big Lake had to be sold harder because it was an ambitious adventure. The lake was twenty-five miles away, and it had to be reached on foot in order to earn the hiking badge. Fifteen of those miles were rugged, too, following trails and rough logging tracks. I'd been to Big Lake once before, when I was twelve. I didn't remember exactly how to get there, but I had a map and a fairly good memory. For me, the biggest attraction of Big Lake was the fishing, which was superb. No road gave access anywhere near the lake, so the fishing was largely undisturbed.

Three of the better scouts were of the right age. At fourteen they were able to pull their own weight, but still too young for high school pleasures. Besides, these scouts had parents who thought I'd be a good influence on them, so I felt reasonably confident when I mentioned my plan to Steve, Randy, and Jon. At first, the mere suggestion of a twenty-five-mile hike sent them hurrying off to the soda fountain to recover. Once they got over the shock, I kept mentioning the huge fish, the great trail, the hiking badge they'd earn. It took a few months, but they took the bait. We agreed to make the trek to Big Lake that summer.

I know, today, some of the things I did wrong. First, I simply told them what we'd need and gave them a list. It was a good start, but we should have set up and tried the actual equipment we planned to use. In those days, you see, camping gear was an assortment of borrowed items, gifts given to kids, and war surplus. Much of it was of questionable value and not really fit for use on the trail.

The second thing I did wrong concerned the food. We pooled our money and gave Steve and Randy the cash and responsibility for coming up with a menu. I should have known better. Steve had a lively humor, the kind inclined to provide smoked oysters and cheese for breakfast or, even worse, for every meal.

At age sixteen, my object wasn't so much to help those three scouts become better campers as it was to get myself back to Big Lake. If they learned a few things, fine, but I didn't give them as much instruction as I gave sales pitch. Wise old bird that I am now, I can see I placed too much emphasis on the *goal*, and not nearly enough emphasis on the *process* of reaching it. In addition, I assumed the other boys were capable and understood my instructions, but then, I assumed I was capable and knowledgeable enough to carry the trip off, as well.

A few weeks after school let out, we were on our way. The day started warm, turned hot, and after a few miles it became muggy and awful. The first five miles went well enough, all things considered, but it wasn't working up to be a swell hike. We were lucky in one sense, though. Seven miles out, we came to the Grouse River. Packs were dropped to the ground and clothing followed, as the four of us cooled off in the shallow, swirling pool below a log bridge. What raw pleasure that was! And what a bloody pain it was to have to leave it! Our clothes felt hot and grimey; our feet felt tender after a long soak. And we'd skinny-dipped far too long, leaving the pool way behind schedule.

I remember it well. Steve had an army surplus pack frame, and his canteen clanged against it with every step. The heat was sweltering, and after leaving the river we had to head into the bush, where the air was held still by the trees. According to the map, we were right on course, but we still had a long way to go. Along that humid forest trail, the miles felt like monsters.

The next landmark came at twelve miles out, where an abandoned railroad grade was a fixed point to follow until we came to Garvey Creek, a few miles farther on. At the grade, we flopped down to rest our burning feet. Our rest break almost turned into a mutiny, but it was as far to go back as it was to go on, so going forward won out. Fortunately, a breeze was coming down the railroad grade, so getting to the creek was slightly more pleasant than the previous miles had been.

From the creek we had ten more miles to go. Also at the creek, we had to locate a footpath and follow it for nearly seven miles before another abandoned railroad grade would take us the remaining distance to Big Lake. I knew the next seven miles would be the worst, because I remembered slogging through this swampy trail on my earlier visit. It was the sort of trail that would make a moose weep in frustration, but under the circumstances I didn't want to mention that to my companions.

The trail was going to be a wet one anyway, so what could have been more appropriate than rain? The heat of the day had led to a cloud build up, and the rain started, quickly building in intensity. Our raingear, borrowed from dads and neighbors, wasn't up to the downpour—mostly, it just didn't fit us. Jon was busy using one hand to hold his rainpants up, and even then he kept tripping over his cuffs.

We continued on, slipping, falling, getting soaking wet, and numbed-crazy by rain continuously drumming on our heads. I recall trying to read the map once, but in the torrent of water the paper was all mush and blur. We staggered along. The rain was a hard-pelting companion, which kept visibility down to a few yards.

It seemed like hours later when we emerged from the swamp and started onto the railroad grade for the final three-mile leg. The rain continued, but at least we were no longer wading in water. Our first view of Big Lake was a relief, but, in retrospect, it was only such relief as a drowning rat might feel, given the chance to drown more slowly.

My three companions, aside from an occasional mutter or groan, were quiet, and I tried to cheer them along for the last few miles. Their reaction was blunt and indicated a deep lack of appreciation for the fun and adventure we were having. But I had a trump card. I told them about the cook shack I'd seen standing on my first visit. Hearing of a cabin, a place to get dry, they rebounded, and we were soon making better time along the lakeshore.

The cook shack I remembered was a wreck, but they didn't know that, not until they saw it. The years since my earier visit had not done the shack any favors. My friends howled in anger and frustration.

I countered by saying, "Well, we came here to camp, didn't we? So, let's break out the shelter halves and make our camp. You don't really want to stay in that cruddy old shack, anyway."

Randy assured me he'd stay *anywhere* where it wasn't raining, but he joined us in removing his shelter half from his pack. Jon had been the one to suggest the use of shelter halves, saying they were lightweight, easy to use, and as good as any pup tent. Steve's shelter half turned out to be an army poncho, of no use as anything but a poncho. Randy's shelter half had buttons, while the halves Jon and I had were equipped with snaps. Only Jon and I had halves that mated, but Jon's half had a big rip down one side. Among the four of us, we didn't have much more than half a tent, and that was being generous.

Our gaze turned to the cook shack. The windows were broken out. The door was torn off. Previous campers had abused the stove; the interior was a shambles. Amazingly, the roof didn't leak, so we moved in, the shack replacing the tents we didn't have.

With a half-rotted broom we cleared off the floor, then set the table back. By luck, we found all the stove parts and were able to put the stove back in workable condition. A double-bed frame with a set of springs sat against one wall. Under it, the previous campers had left a small supply of dry wood. Jon's torn shelter half was cut into pieces and nailed over the window holes. Steve's poncho replaced the door. We had a place to stay.

We also had a few problems. As it grew dark, the rain continued and the mosquitoes came in droves. In order to conserve on dry wood, we had to search for other wood outdoors. Two cooked while two tried to drag in wood that might burn. In time, we got a good fire going, and even the wet wood could be kept burning hotly. To keep the mosquitoes out, we had to keep the door and windows covered. The interior grew warm, and we rediscovered how wet we were. We'd already discovered that everything in our packs was soaked, and we had our extra clothes and sleeping bags spread out to dry. The interior of the shack looked like a laundry and felt like a sweatbox.

Still, it was better than being in the rain. We sat down to eat, feeling darn glad to be indoors. In order to dry things out we kept the stove burning, the interior of the shack growing warmer still. Sweating and uncomfortably aware of the oppressive weight of our wet clothes, we were soon adding what we wore to the items set out to dry. It went like an addiction—the first grubby, wet item taken off felt so good that we were soon stripped to the skin, spreading everything out to dry and enjoying the heat. We finished our meal in the nude, no doubt making a few crude comments about who had the biggest appetite.

In the steamy interior, our clothing and sleeping bags felt as wet as when we'd started. And although we needed the heat to dry things out, the same heat was cooking us like limp noodles. Of course, we could have opened the door flap and let in some fresh air—along with a cloud of opportunistic mosquitoes, which could hardly have had better luck than to find themselves in an enclosed area with four bare, sweaty boys. We endured the heat as long as possible, then let in some fresh air and another swarm of skeeters. It kept us occupied, anyway.

Several hours of that and we were exhausted. It was past midnight, the the humid heat in the shack wasn't letting anything dry. We'd used up the good wood, so the stove sizzled, smoked, and slow-cooked us. In desperation, we threw down three wet sleeping bags to cover the bed springs and used one unzipped bag as a blanket. We realized we'd never fit on the bed lengthwise, so we agreed to sleep with our feet hanging off the side. It was the best we could do, the floor being far too dirty, wet, and foul to sleep on.

I remember putting out the candle, then the feel of crawling onto a drippy-wet pile of sleeping bags. An equally damp bag served as a blanket, while on either side of me Steve and Randy's radiant, bare flesh added to the heat. It was an awful (beyond words) night. Miserably hot, I wanted to toss and turn, but couldn't without disturbing one boy or the other. Flesh covered by the sleeping bag was hot and wet. Flesh exposed was mosquito food. The bare legs were a lost cause.

Half-awake, uncomfortable beyond words, angry as hell; the four of us tried to find a comfortable position for sleep, which eluded us until near dawn when exhaustion took over. We slept, then, in a huddle, no longer conscious of propriety. The predawn chill had made us cold and wet, so we'd quietly squeezed together on the bed, finding warmth and escape from the pesty mosquitoes.

That slumbering state accounted for three hours. So short a respite, only to be ended, rudely, by another sodden day. The rain continued; we groped our way through a soggy breakfast and argued about whether we should go or stay. By lunch we still hadn't decided, but then the decision was made for us. The rain came down almost as heavily as the day before, and we were pretty sure we'd never get out before dark with conditions like that. We stayed.

Again wrapped up in wet, dirty clothes, we went about the task of making our "camp" more comfortable. Our first need was more wood to burn. Working in the rain, sweating as we chopped, we were soon as wet and dirty as we'd been the day before. We were barely holding our own against the elements. We'd almost get a pair of socks dried when one of us, by accident, would bump them, the socks ending up in a puddle on the floor, wet again. And even if we got the socks dry, they didn't stay that way more than a few minutes in the rain.

We hauled in a mountain of wet wood, nursed a hot fire into life, and watched the cabin heat up while we slow-cooked in our squishy outfits. I guess what happened next was inevitable. Muttering a curse, Jon leapt from his chair and began to unbutton, unbelt, and unzip. Angrily, he threw each stripped-away item at his feet. Naked, he jumped up and down on the pile, which oozed water with each jump. Then, a wild look in his eye, he threw himself on our table and screamed, "Come and eat me you lousy bugs!! Bring your knife and fork! I can't stand the slow torture anymore, so eat me! Get it over with!!"

Our shack filled again with laundry. Everything was as wet and ugly as it had been yesterday, except for the sleeping bags, which were slightly improved. Not so our moods. We joined Jon in bareness almost as a defiant gesture. If the life was going to be sucked from us by flying insects, we'd go down together.

Somehow, knowing what the night was going to be like didn't help. We put off retiring as long as possible. We swapped tales while swatting bugs between bouts of sweating and cooling off. Slaphappy-tired, we crawled into bed in an awake stupor. Dazed, we ignored our discomfort as we jockeyed into positions resembling sleep, which didn't come until dawn's chill forced us into a sleeping truce.

We woke bleary-eyed and worn down to rote behaviors. After a dull and damp breakfast, we began to fill our packs. Our packing would have won no prizes for neatness. Socks, soaking wet and crusted with mud, went into the pack along with sleeping bag and toothbrush.

Our feet, wet for days, blistered easily because the flesh was bath-tender. Our moods on the hike out swung wildly from jubilation at leaving to snappy anger at the least annoyance. We limped home, our trip to Big Lake ending a day early, complete with light drizzle.

Shortly after the trip—that fall, I believe—Jon, Randy, and Steve dropped out of scouts. They told me it wasn't anything personal, just that they couldn't handle any more outdoor "rewards." Anyway, Randy wanted to spend more time playing basketball instead of camping, so dropping out was a natural change, as the trio was often seen shooting baskets together.

The following summer, though, Steve rejoined me for a canoe trip down a lonely stretch of river. We had a good time, and along the way we talked often about our Big Lake trip, finding that some of the same things had occurred to us or happened to us as a result. We made a good camping team, and it was a pleasant time of consolidation as well as discovery. I had to agree with Steve about one thing, too. Like him, I was darn glad this trip was in a canoe. To tell the truth, I've never felt the same about backpacking since the expedition to Big Lake. It was a swan song in the rain.

The Hunt

I'd yet to turn eleven when we moved north and I entered grade seven, an ex-Chicago boy, head brimming with woodsy dreams. Large for my age, I doubt the other boys knew how much in awe I was of their experience or how afraid of them I was, as both newcomer and outsider. They were rough, forthright, country boys, and I was unused to their direct style. They would often ask personal questions and seemed to have large circles of friends. A city-bred boy like me was used to being more cautious with people, and, outside of close family, one normally had few friends, except for small, closed groups.

Into this new world, I tried to fit myself. In art class, I drew a plaid-jacketed figure, which was soon vandalized. In shop, I made a moose wall-plaque of plywood. In English, I read outdoor stories for my book reports. I wanted to become part of my neighbors' world as fully and quickly as possible.

Yet, I was often turned away — if not by them, then by my own reactions. I was greatly shocked to hear my peers openly talk of sexual adventures and experiments. It was a further shock to observe their eagerness to smoke and use vulgar language. As soon as no adult was present or within range, even the nicest lads in school turned into accomplished gutter crawlers. And the first time in the showers after gym was another awakening. Comments flew back and forth as we were sized-up and made prey to a host of raunchy comments, some of which probably were clever, but I was too embarrassed to notice. It was enough to cause me to keep my own company, except for *one* thing: The start of school announced the coming of fall. Days grew cooler, leaves began to turn, and to all the boys this meant the hunting season was approaching.

Hunting talk was a relief from their usual smutty fare. It was also exactly what I was after as a North Woods activity. I listened closely to learn all I could of something I'd had no chance to try in Chicago. The first hunting of the year was what the boys called "Pat'Ridge Huntin' ". They meant, of course, partridge or ruffed grouse, as I learned from a guidebook borrowed from the library. The boys raved about what fun hunting "pat'ridge" was and how good "pat'ridge" was to eat. From their comments, I learned that some preferred to use a small-gauge shotgun (the 410 being most common), while other boys scorned such "easy huntin'" and bragged that only a head shot with a 22-caliber rifle would really do. In a catalog I found nice 410 shotguns and pretty, new 22 rifles, all well beyond my allowance.

Determined, though, I asked around and found a neighbor with an old 22 to sell. The elderly man wanted five dollars. I felt certain I could become a good enough shot to bring home my meat with this kind of weapon, and I had five dollars left over from helping tourists with their fishing. I knew that my mother had only one association with guns, and that was: Guns go with crooks. Then, too, our business wasn't doing well, and I was sure that neither of my parents would approve of my spending five dollars for something nonessential. Practical concerns didn't stop me, however, they simply slowed me down and caused me to hide the gun in the garage after I bought it.

Secretly, I went out to practice marksmanship. I soon learned that a box of ammunition didn't last long if you weren't careful. With economy as a prod, I buckled down and grew able to hit targets with reasonable success. Shortly after my proficiency improved, I made my first kill.

Walking home along a wooded path through the balsams after a practice session, I heard a red squirrel chatter. It happened almost as you imagine it, a sudden urge, an opportunity—I acted automatically while trembling with anticipation. Overhead the squirrel chattered, I took aim, squeezed, the bolt snapped, shell fired, the red squirrel halted in mid-chatter, it slumped forward on the branch, then tumbled free, brushing other branch-tips, continuing down until it landed at my feet, white belly-fur up. I was sickened by what I'd done. I'd killed to no purpose, and at that moment I'd have given anything to undo the deed.

Shaking, I rushed away, the little 22 feeling heavier than it had before. In the garage, while I cleaned it, I saw the gun in a new way. The weapon was now invested with power, but there was a feeling of sadness and unfairness connected with such power. In an uneven contest, the gun had taken a life and was dispassionate toward the entire process. Looking at it, it hardly seemed possible. It was a crudely simple, cheap, ugly little gun with a "bargain" stock of yellow birch and a cocking knob painted red. Most of the blueing had been worn off, causing the gun to look almost toylike, as if it were made of cast metal. Yet, this unpretentious weapon had, with my unthinking help, killed what I had directed it to. As I cleaned it, the smell of solvent filling my nose, I promised myself never again to kill for that kind of sport. From then on, I'd kill for meat and use what I killed, the respectable form of hunting.

I waited for the hunting season to begin, but I was well aware that many of the local fellows had already started. From the way they talked, I was afraid there'd be no grouse left in the woods, but I was determined to begin my hunting right. When the official opening day came, I left the garage and headed into the thick woods that surrounded our house. In the distance I heard the hollow reports of shotguns where carloads of hunters road-hunted. But on my path in the woods it was different. I followed silent moss-covered trails that clung to the lay of the land. I kept low and tried to be as much a "hunter" as possible.

I had a good day, lots of walking and activity, but in thick woods, hunting is no easy matter. Game has ample cover, and several times, a ruffled grouse exploded from hiding a few feet away, each time giving me more fright than opportunity. By late afternoon, though, I came upon one bird that strutted back and forth, clucking. I took aim and dropped it with a head shot. As soon as I'd fired, another bird flew off, leaving me with the realization that I'd only seen one of a pair of birds, the obvious one.

Carrying my bird by the legs, I walked home. On the way I felt both proud and letdown. I was glad to have achieved something, but I felt sad about killing one bird of a pair.

At home, the bird and I were promptly rushed outside. "You killed it, so you clean it." Down by the lake, I proceeded to dress that meat, much as an eleven year old would clean a fish. I remember being aghast at the visceral stink inside the cavity. But most of all, I was amazed by how many feathers there were to pluck. My hands were like ice and it was getting dark by the time I'd finished and was able to return to the house, a trailing whirl of down accompanying me.

Inside there was a *discussion* of where the bird came from, and where the gun came from (I'd slipped up in my haste to show off). My parents, though stern, allowed as how "what's done is done." My mother called a neighbor lady to find out how to cook partridge.

We ate it the next day. My parents agreed it was awful. I decided I didn't mind the taste, which was strong, but I had a vested interest to protect. To be honest, the bird tasted slightly of turpentine, and I recalled from cleaning it that its crop had been filled with pine needles. Later I learned that the locals call such birds spruce hens. They are considered inedible because of their feed. They are also reputed to be the stupidest of birds, ridiculously easy to kill. When I learned these things, my rank as hunter slipped by more than a few degrees.

I hunted partridge a few other times that first year, improving as a hunter. In later years, I hunted only from time to time, more out of habit than need or desire. I liked the feel of a gun in my hand as I walked through cool, fall days. I liked the time of year, and hunting was a good excuse for wandering about.

What, you may ask, cooled my ardor to hunt? Was it the spruce hen or some sadness over killing? It was neither. Instead, something replaced the importance of hunting. Something more powerfully urgent crept in. I fell in love, completely, with a sensation I'd never encountered before.

Above our house a half-mile or so, the balsam forest gave way to a rise covered in aspen. Beneath the aspen, in open terrain where the sun reached, the ground was covered with alders, raspberry, thimbleberry, timothy grass, large leaf aster. Take those things after they've gone past-ripe and mingle them with the air of a cool, damp day—it creates the purest perfume of autumn. I walked into that glade and was assaulted by an aroma that put hunting to shame. It was as if that odor summed up the meaning of life in the forest, making perfume of dying leaves. It was like finding a trusted friend in an alien place.

None of the local boys had ever mentioned the overpowering pungency of the forest in autumn. They'd talked of bag limits and good times with their buddies. Rarely, one of them might say it was "nice" in the woods. From all angles I could see there was considerable mystique connected with hunting, but no one had told me about an olfactory sensation that would lay siege to my soul. The only thing like it, also a new sensation at that age, new-found sexuality which formed a core of impression both promising and frightening, reality muffled in secrecy.

Why mix the imagery of such personal and secret experience with the innocence of a natural perfume? Partly because the power of each is similar: sensual enough to be sexual and electric enough to be erotic. It is like the heightened, trembling response one feels toward a loved one. Their presence triggers mental and physical reactions. So it was that my encounter with fall was like an interlude with a woodland wraith. So it is, too, that much of hunting is padded with hidden messages, and I have simply called upon one of the most obvious.

It did not, of course, become obvious all at once. In order to discover the experience, I had to leave the path. Holding the little 22 safely above the damp foliage, I waded into the stiff stalks and oversized leaves of thimbleberry. Like vegetable arms, the stalks held back my legs, the leaves making a heavy rustling sound as I pushed ahead.

Then I reached the clearing, dominated by the tall aspens, nearly bare of all leaves except for a very few clinging to high branches. Passing winds would rattle the leaves, making clear the reason for the name "quaking aspen." Other leaves, giving way to vegetable fatigue, would fall, hitting the dry branches, making a whispered rattle, then joining the ranks of fallen leaves on the ground. Yellow-gold aspen leaves formed a ground cover as intricate as the most elaborate Persian rug.

In this gold-floored clearing, a few tag alders formed bent-over clumps, near which a stray thimbleberry or raspberry had migrated from below and taken hold. The raspberry in fall is a thing to be avoided, its stem dry and spiky, the leaves still holding firm, russett red, but less vivid than the fruit that had clung to the plant weeks earlier. Here and there across the clearing, feathery heads of timothy grass holding seeds, nodded on threadlike stems. These grass filaments catch on boot or cuff and are carried away by the hunter, who acts as a sower of seed.

Walking here, the gold leaves shuffled with each step, but there was another rustle as well. The fallen leaves had nearly covered the large leaf aster, which made a deeper sound when disturbed. Where I had created a path the gold leaves were pushed aside, leaving a green road of exposed aster leaves. I'll always remember and honor the aster for staying green well into fall. My school friends called the aster, "Lumberjack's Ass Wipe," because of its abundance and large leaves. I wondered why they didn't recognize its beauty and instead gave it such a vulgar name.

Having described the scene, having mentally walked a quartering course up the slope, I can provide a partial picture of the sight and sound. I've too little means of capturing the smell, however. Crisp and damp like autumn, it held wafted scents of sweet berries, the tang of gold leaves, the subtle aroma of aspen bark, carried on winds lightly tinted with resinous balsam from the lower slopes. All this perfume lay in the air, alive, palpable, and trembling like the leaves that rattled on the trees.

The Walk

The earliest of early-winter,
no snow transforms the waiting time,
with its patches of sunlit warmth
and richly aromatic woods smells
followed in moments by the chill
of a cloud shadow and a rattling wind,
its teeth nibbling the edges
of a too-light jacket.

On such a day, I walk with a friend
along treebound aisles, through open spaces,
following a path, walking, no destination.
It is the sort of thing I do
too seldom, foolishly preferring to keep
my problems to myself, keeping
my joys in secrecy, too.

But my walk with a friend
is not philosophy time.
We do, in fact, nothing important, of moment.
Discussion or debate do not
spill from our lips. Rather,
we see trees growing in clumps,
rocks tumbled side to side,
all the shoulder-to-shoulder life of a forest.
The medium its own message.

Yet, how strangely we come to view life.
In our personal lives, life's offerings,
we see as trials. Caught in action,
we fret to spend time nonurgently.
It's difficult for us to do nothing,
like these trees, teammates of the forest.
Scurrying to catch the notes, like fallen leaves,
we often do not hear the song.

Early winter brings an early night.
The moon's above the trees,
a few stars begin to show. From here,
we're sure they are "stars," but
if we went closer, passing through
swirling dusts of time and space,
would our "star" be star, galaxy, universe?
My perspective changed, small points are huge,
yesterday's pressing concern a dust mote.

While walking with a friend,
doing nothing especially significant or grand,
a part of me catches the chorus
of universe to time,
the chant of galaxy to galaxy,
following the time-line of space,
with tree-to-tree applause and review.
Without realizing or reasoning,
I walk to that music, happy/uplifted.

I can wonder how long the universe
has sung its song to us,
how long it has spun and painted
the spiral scenes with lyrics, wordless,
which reach us even here.
It is a mystery as simply complex
as entering a forest clearing—
my shadow flickers in the wind-tossed grass,
it runs with the wind waves, light and dark,
it runs, to be lost forever;
shadows in the running, weaving stems,
gone, yet ever-present.

Logger

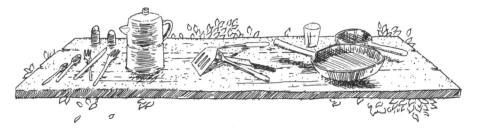

It had taken me nearly two hours to locate and reach Ron's clearing off the forest service tote-road. I recognized his pickup and parked my Land Rover next to his Dodge.

Getting out, I smelled woodsmoke. There was aspen burning, the smell of it thick, almost sweet. Even at the time, I was struck by the way living in the area had taught me to recognize things like the smell of a particular kind of wood being burned. Ron had set up a tiny, airtight, sheet metal stove and three lengths of stovepipe. It almost looked ridiculous to see a stove set up in the open, seemingly serving no function. But nearby were a pair of sawhorses with boards laid across them to act as a table top. This was Ron's kitchen. A coffeepot, other pans, and silverware lay on the golden, rough-sawn boards. This "logging kitchen" appeared vulnerable and exposed, but Ron had taken the simplest, most functional path for his eating place.

I think I can tell quite a lot about a person from the way they conduct themselves in the bush. I don't mean "daylight" people, though. A "daylight" person is one who works in or uses the bush by day, but returns to a home and friends after dark. Daylight users don't live in the bush, not as Ron did. He only came to town once or twice a week for fuel and supplies. He'd spent much of his life living in and around forest clearings like this one.

I had plenty of time to look at Ron's style of bush life and think things over, because Ron was operating his "Jonnie" dozer and wasn't yet aware of my presence. He was concentrating on leveling an area and removing a pair of stubborn stumps. Watching him work, I caught a hint of pattern or method as he kept his dozer in almost constant motion. I could tell he'd spent many hours like this during his life. Operating the machine was an extension of his personal self.

Unlike those of other loggers, Ron's dozer was clean. I could see places where he'd touched up the paint. He kept the machine looking good, and as I continued to watch, it hit me that the clean look of the dozer was matched by the clean sound of the way Ron ran it. He kept to a steady, rhythmic pace that didn't die off or indulge in ear-thudding bursts.

About then, Ron noticed me and shot a quick nod and gesture in my direction. But he didn't stop work just then. He apparently intended to finish some task while he was at it, and as I continued to wait, I wondered how many such clearings would define or measure Ron's life. Though I didn't know him well, I knew Ron was always starting a new project. He thrived on beginning sawmills and opening fresh logging sales. Work was his life, and he was a hard worker. I guessed he had to be over seventy, so he had a good fifty years more experience than I, something I respected.

It was partly Ron's age and experience that had brought me to visit him. When I'd seen him in town, he'd told me he was having trouble with the brakes on a truck like one I'd once had. It was partly whim and partly respect that made me volunteer to fix the brakes. Very matter-of-factly, he'd said, "Sure," but I had the feeling he didn't believe I meant it. But then, Ron wasn't an easy person to know or figure out. He was most often alone and had apparently never mentioned "family" to anyone. Ron had simply shown up in the area when he was a young man, and he had lived a solitary working life ever since. Some people said he'd probably fled his real home after getting some girl pregnant or getting into trouble with the law. I preferred to think that a more touching tragedy had caused him to leave and not glance back.

But there was no way to find out and I would not have dared the rudeness of asking. Ron shut his dozer off. In the fresh silence, he crossed the black soil he'd recently exposed, his arms swinging in rhythm with his slow, unusual, loping walk.

When he got close enough, I stated my purpose, mostly to break my own tension about having invited myself. "H'lo, Ron. Brought my tools so I can work on those brakes for you. Where've you got that truck?"

"I forgot you said you'd do that," he commented, and I could tell he was surprised to see me there, tools and all. "C'mon," he said with a head jerk, and he led me along his new logging road while he whistled softly under his breath. After a hundred yards and two corners, I saw the truck.

Ron pointed, "Truck's over there. Spare parts are back where I been workin', but you'll have to take it apart first, anyways. Even if you don't finish today, it'll still help to have it started." He left me to work alone. In a while, I heard his dozer running again.

He'd already jacked the truck up and set it on blocking. For his convenience or mine, I wondered? Once I crawled under and began working, though, my mind wasn't idly speculating. I was too busy with short-focus tasks and solving immediate problems to ponder personal concerns. Deep in the mind, personal reactions continue to cook, but during work a person is usually too occupied to notice.

Turned out that I didn't finish the job that day. Ron was missing one brake hose, so I couldn't bleed and test the system for him. He'd have to take care of that on his own, a tricky, sometimes mean job for one person. But without that hose there was no way to complete the job.

It was late afternoon when I told Ron where the project stood. He nodded in agreement over the steps I'd taken, and had the same kind of "wouldn't you know it" reaction about the one missing hose that I did. To insure a speedy final repair, I gave him the bad hose so he could match it exactly.

The light was getting weak, and the cold started to set in. Once or twice a minute, a breeze would stir through the trees and deliver a few leaves to the area Ron had left bare and clear. The fallen birch leaves were like gold doubloons resting on black velvet.

"I was about ready to take a break," said Ron, "so, c'mon, sit down, and have some coffee; warm y'self up." He led me to his outdoor kitchen, where he produced a cup from a much-used brown paper sack.

"The cup's clean," Ron laughed. "That's just sawdust on it. Workin' logging you get used to having sawdust in everything. It's clean dirt, don't worry."

Taking sips of Ron's black brew, I listened to him tell me how he was trying to lay this "yard" out so logs could be easily delivered and unloaded to a new portable mill he'd bought.

"You used to guide up here before the war, didn't you?" I asked.

"Yeh. Long time ago. Lots of rich tourists back then wanted a man to pack and cook for 'em. They fished, had fun, while you worked. But them "babes in the woods" were damn glad to have you. They'd be pretty decent about it, you know. They'd 'a been sunk without me, get it?"

I nodded, "How come you quit guiding?"

Ron gave a cross between a snort and a chuckle. "People changed, for one thing. After the war, those rich doctors, lawyers, professors quit comin' up. Folks with less money started comin' on their own, bringin' their own equipment and such, too. Hell, today, how could a grown man make any livin' guiding with only kids to guide for? Anyway, logging got in my blood, so I'm workin' in the woods. I can be happy about that."

After a pause, Ron asked, "How much I owe you for today?"

"Forget it, Ron," I said, "I just did it for the hell of it. You know, a good excuse to get away for a while."

He gave me a sideways look. "That don't happen too often. How come you don't want nothin'?"

"Ron," I said, being serious, "it gave me an excuse to get away from my own projects. Know how sometimes your own projects wear you down, but somebody else's work is easy to do? Instead of beating my head against a wall at home, I got to be outside on a nice fall day. Besides, I want to see that old truck of yours keep ticking. Those were good trucks, right?"

He nodded, "Yeh. And it's nice to be able to work in the woods, too. Best kind of work there is. I forget how lucky I am, then someone like you who has to work in town all the time comes along and reminds me."

A breeze rattled more leaves onto the floor of the logging yard, the wind still scented with smoke from Ron's outdoor kitchen. I spat out a woodchip from my last swallow of Ron's coffee, then stood and shook his hand. My nose was tingling from the cold, and I wasn't dressed for sitting still outdoors. It was time to go.

He followed me to the Rover, and before I got in, he gave me an awkward but sincere "Thanks!" Then he turned to amble off, arms swinging, whistling softly under his breath. If it hadn't been for his isolation, I'd have thought him one of the luckiest men alive. Even so, I drove away feeling he was more fortunate than I.

The Bridge

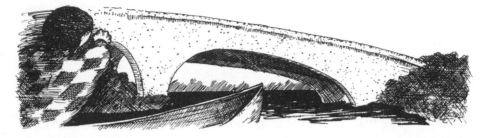

When you spend enough time in the bush, certain places stand out in memory like landmarks on the heart's topography. One route I have fond memories of begins on YH Lake. (I won't give locational data other than initials, because the important thing isn't the "where" so much as the "feel" of the place—with luck, you'll find your own places to fit this sort of description). You start from a spruce-lined bay and quickly have to fight a stiff sidewind as the course bends left out of the bay and down to the corner of the lake. After a few minutes of brisk paddling the first portage is reached.

The portage starts at an outcrop of white granite that forms a low rise. If a person had to pick a representative portage, this one would do nicely on any postcard or calendar. The path is well worn and crosses the granitic dome that forces the river feeding the lake into a narrow cascade, impossible to paddle. Again, it's only a matter of a few minutes and the portage is crossed, its upper end leaving the paddler at a still-water landing on a tiny, shoestring lake.

Paddling out, you're not sure if you're crossing a lake or a river. At places the shore meets the water's edge with a sharp line of cliffs and trees, as can be found on most lakes. But a little farther along, the shoreline is nothing but boggy acres buzzing with insects and noisy with red-wing blackbirds, as if you were moving along a lazy river. The river/lake shifts its emphasis from minute to minute until it begins to broaden, signaling the entrance to the next lake.

SF is the next lake, and its shores are thickly grown in black spruce. From a canoe it's difficult to tell how hardy the trees are, but the first campsite is on an island that has some of the largest and most robust black spruce I've ever seen. The entire site is musky with the accumulated scent of spruce needles, which thickly cover the ground with a rust-colored robe that dampens noise and perfumes the air. Past the island the lake gets wider, and near its widest portion there is another campsite set on a breadloaf dome of light granite. I once watched a nearly perfect sunset frame itself against that site.

Less than a mile from that campsite, SF Lake merges into J Lake in a long, narrow passage filled with canoe-catching rocks. One of my young assistants called such boulders "aluma rocks" because they bore so much aluminum decoration scratched off passing canoes. I'm sure there is some logical place where SF Lake becomes J Lake in that narrows, but I've always been too busy avoiding rocks to notice where that point might be.

After so much careful navigation to enter it, J Lake is something of a disappointment. The lake sits in a broad, shallow dish and offers few prominent features. Trees slope gently away from the water. There are no cliffs or huge rocks set at the water's edge. A narrow fringe of reeds marks the line where the water becomes too deep for them. Unlike most of our northern lakes, J is quite uniform, almost a perfect average between a rocky lake and a boggy, weedy one. I've noted a few campsites on J, and when I've examined them I was able to tell they'd been used by fishing parties. Our fisherfolk seem to pick up some quite nice pike on J, but I've never been interested enough in fishing to be willing to spend a night there feeding the bugs.

As dull as it is, J Lake is a perfect prelude to J Creek, which is like taking a trip on something left over from glacial times. The creek is hardly two canoes wide, and it is full of snakelike twists. Much of the bottom is muskeg, which seems to drag at the canoe, but in a few places low cliffs confine the water on either side until the bog dominates again. Against one of these cliffs there is a large beaver lodge, standing a good six feet out of the water. The combination of thick muskeg swamp and moss-covered cliffs in a tight, little valley creates a sort of primal feel to J Creek and makes me think that this tiny body of water is an ancestral pathway forming a bond between rock-bound and swamp-bound territories.

J Creek ends at the base of a cliff, where the water flowing into it seeps from a collection of fissures that mark the upper end of the flowage. From here it's a longish and steep portage to reach GJ Lake, which is notable for its steep shores and rugged, wild look. Cliffs and tall trees begin at the water's edge, and there seems to be hardly a shallow spot anywhere on the lake. Lake bottom can only be seen close to shore before it becomes lost in the steeply plunging deeps. There is a modest little campsite on the lake, just before the portage to W Lake. I stayed there once when I was forced to do so by heavy storms, but the entire time I felt penned in by the walls that tightly form the lake.

That feeling does not persist after carrying the portage to W, which is a large and open lake. Its highlands and cliffs are set against backgrounds of low hills amid a broad panorama. The big lakes lend themselves more to open landscapes and heavy winds. After paddling on smaller, enclosed lakes, W makes you want to get out and really paddle, to run down the lake, speeding along its vistas. The eye catches glimpses of sandy coves and jutting promontories that shelter globular bays with still, dark waters. W is a lovely lake, and above it I've often seen eagles in their airy circuit of patrol.

Aside from it's beauty, though, I'll always have another reason for remembering W. The first time I paddled it I was using a map with an error. The map clearly showed a portage into a small lake at its extreme southwest corner, and from there another portage to the river. There was, indeed, a portage to the tiny lake, which lay in a cliffy depression that defied the creation of any path leading farther. None the less, I carefully searched every inch of the lake, then backtracked to W and combed its shore along the southwest corner, looking for that elusive portage to the river. Several hours later I headed to the northwest corner of the lake and soon discovered the river I'd been trying so hard to locate. Access to the river didn't even require a portage, and I settled back to enjoy travel on its wide and pleasant course.

Actually, river travel near the Boundary Waters isn't all that pleasant. Since rivers have to flow, that also means they have to drop, following a gradient, and that means that sooner or later (more likely sooner and more often) the river will lead directly to a portage. You're lucky to go three miles on a river without hitting some sort of rapids or portage. On lakes it's fairly common to go six or seven miles at a shot before having to portage. Our rivers, therefore, require more work, but it's still a welcome change of pace to paddle one of the bigger rivers. They usually provide more wildlife contact, thus making up for the nuisance of portaging.

The first portage on the W river, though, is one that makes you take notice. There's a tiny landing just above a fairly high and jagged waterfall. You have to stay just at the edge of the current and quickly latch onto the only possible place to land, a rock that slants into the water at a 50 to 60-degree angle. It's a treacherous landing, and if you miss it or slip off it you come perilously close to getting into the full sweep of current tearing over the falls. There's one little cedar tree growing out of the rock there, and I've been thankful for it a number of times.

That portage past, the river settles down for a while and the paddler can relax and enjoy. One of the finest sights along this stretch is the osprey nesting. Their large nest is first visible in the distance as a dark spot in a mature pine. You notice that spot because the adult birds come and go from it. As the river brings you closer, the size of the nest and birds becomes more obvious — an osprey is nearly as large as a golden eagle. Beyond the nesting site, the most commonly seen attraction on the river is the "crippled duck" who leads you away from her young. There is also the occasional otter who, if startled, will hiss and bark at you, giving a sharp warning.

Paddling, making frequent portages, and watching the wildlife is all very nice, but it's also tiring. After enough time on the river one's thoughts turn to campsites and a chance to rest on shore. On all of the W river there is one really super little campsite. It's located in the middle of the next portage alongside an impressive natural chute, where you can fall asleep to the nearby rumble of a river on the move.

You know you're nearing this special campsite when you see the first sign of the approaching portage. A few rocks begin to show along the river's edge, and there is a visible narrowing of the river as it approaches the tree-covered rock feature that necessitates the portage. When you're really close you can see the current picking up, and then just before the landing there's a narrow skiff-like island in the flow. As soon as that bit of island is passed you can see the landing off on the right side.

At least you used to be able to see it. The last time I paddled around that island I was hit by an entirely new sight. There was a concrete bridge abutment where the landing used to be, a bridge spanning the river, and as I watched, a truckload with logs roared over the bridge leaving a yellow cloud of dust and the faint smell of diesel fuel.

Aside from being shocked (all the while hoping the bridge wasn't real) I had the most awful sinking feeling I'd ever experienced. I felt as though something ancient was being destroyed, stripped away. It's hard to put into words. I remembered what Sigurd Olson had to say about the road going into Saganaga. He'd come to grips with civilization encroaching on Saganaga back in the mid-fifties, and he wrote about it in *The Singing Wilderness*. I remembered the big fuss about the road crossing Finn Lake in the Portal Zone of the Boundary Waters. That incident was one of the first I had become involved with, back in the mid-sixties. Intellectually I was prepared to cope with roads encroaching on wild country, but when my turn came around to experience it in the mid-seventies, well, I sat in my canoe and just felt awful, dumbfounded, sick, and almost angry that such a thing could happen to a place I loved.

As far as I was concerned, that place in the bush was still wilderness. The road was a cheater's way of getting there. That splendid bridge looked about as appropriate for the bush as would a set of Royal Doulton in a bush rat's knapsack. It simply didn't belong there—but it was there, sure enough.

As my emotions calmed I was able to salvage more from the experience. The nice campsite along the river hadn't been disturbed. The sound of the river covered up most of the occasional truck noise. The area was compromised, but not ruined or despoiled. Indeed, the road would likely make it possible for more people to enjoy the spot, and that would serve the good of society, wouldn't it?

With that question we arrive at one of the central dilemmas concerning wilderness. If experiencing wilderness were simply a matter of scenery or of being on a particular spot, then car camping could qualify as a sort of wilderness travel. But the wilderness experience as I understand it is very much part of a process. It's a combination of attitude and method, and under the best circumstances it involves the harmonious blending of person and place. Wilderness travel has to take time and effort; it must be worked at, just as a relationship must be worked at and desired. As a person seemingly struggles and moves at a snail's pace, there is really an important process taking place. At this slower pace, more particular detail is clear and more time is spent working together with people. There is no quick and easy road to discovering what wilderness has to offer.

I won't make a plea to preserve all wilderness from logging. There is a need both for adequate wilderness areas and for ample supplies of forest products for our society. How the give and take of meeting those needs should work isn't for me alone to decide. But experience compels me to include the warning that wilderness is easily lost, and once it's lost it's pretty much gone for good. We have the ability to open up large tracts of land, and we can do so with astonishing speed. The rest of my canoe trip that week was often followed by the sound of logging skidders operating in the adjoining forests. A huge new area had been opened to harvest, and thousands of acres were involved in the course of a few summers—a clear example of how we can impact large parcels of land with relative ease. Such speedy alteration is anathema to wilderness style, wilderness philosophy, and to wilderness itself.

Seen One Big Tree . . .

Never thought I'd ever have use for a line like that, but there it is. I'll tell you how I came to write it. A few years ago my foster brother who lives in California invited me to become his son's godfather. Accepting, I went West for family reasons and to enjoy a brief vacation; I was five years old the last time I was in California.

Everything went fine. It was nice to see Tom again, and his wife was a delight. Little Stephen was all that could be expected and did a commendable job of complaining, loudly, when water was poured on him at the christening. My other foster brother, Jim, attended with his wife, Rosalba, and it was quietly pleasing to see all of them doing well. Overseeing the event were Tom and Jim's parents, neither of whom speak good English. It was apparent from their faces, however, that they were proud and happy, celebrating this occasion, enjoying the moment, and thankful to have the family back together after years of exile. (When Tom and Jim first came from Cuba to live with us there was little hope that they would ever be able to see their parents again.) Mrs. Diaz wasn't able to say much to me, but the special tamales she made, the old way, wrapped in corn husks by hand, told me how important this occasion was for her.

So, there sat your north woods guide in northern California enjoying new scenes and soaking up a bit of Spanish-speaking culture. It was so different from my turf that I found that even the smallest detail caught my attention. I was captivated, too, when I learned how the hide and tallow trade conducted by Spain via the missions developed in a pattern similar to that of the fur trade controlled by the English in the north woods region. The information was new, but the pattern was familiar and gave me reason for speculation.

The Diaz family knew, of course, of my compulsive love of the outdoors. Tom and Jim had seen me head off to go camping when any sane person would have stayed home. As a special treat for me, they suggested that we take a day and journey to the Muir Woods so I could enjoy a bit of nature and the outdoors.

A fine idea. Little did I know what the outcome would be. Nothing from my past could have prepared me for my reaction. Not that there is anything wrong with Muir Woods, mind you. The trees are big, impressive, beautiful. The paved paths are necessary to protect the immediate environment from destruction. The fences are needed to keep people from trampling the surroundings. The little rest stops and benches are all useful additions along the guided pathways. There's not a thing wrong with Muir Woods, but I almost went out of my mind with boredom. We walked from tree to tree, gazed from trunk to tree top, nodded appreciatively, and so on. Then, out of nowhere I found myself thinking, "Seen one big tree and you've seen them all." I felt quite shocked to find myself reacting that way—believe me, I was no fan of Jim Watt. I couldn't wait until we got out of there.

Of course, my rection was partly due to the circumstances—my vacation didn't begin with any plan on my part to explore the California coastal redwoods. I didn't go West with the thought of looking at trees, regardless of how big they were. I'm around trees all the time, so I'm used to having them enter my thinking, and, to tell the truth, I found it hard to take trees that big seriously; they were more like freaks than useful companions. Trees that big just didn't have a place in my mental scheme of things.

I was reminded, too, of what it is I particularly enjoy about my time in the north woods. I appreciate the trees, waters, rocks, and plants, all of which are essential to the area. But when I go into the woods I almost always hope to *do* something. I will hike, paddle, camp, explore, fish, or ski. It is integrated activity in some form or other. In the setting of the north woods I can be directly, intimately involved with the environment. When I engage in wilderness-style camping I see myself as part of that environment, and I am actively doing something. Walking an asphalt trail in the

Muir Woods just didn't compare. It didn't even come close; like observing Halley's Comet while holding a loved one's hand, I know the difference between a rare and unusual show and something that touches the heart. I came back home to the north woods more ready than ever to embrace it, preferring simple, honest love to the grandest of lofty designs.

Postscript

When first written, the above piece was little more than an idle observation. I was struck by the irony of my reaction to the big redwoods. Since I first wrote those few paragraphs, my initial impression has grown to become a more complete and finished thought.

The difference between a capsuled experience such as the Muir Woods and wilderness camping in the Boundary Waters is one of involvement. In the Muir Woods one is a visitor; in the Boundary Waters one is a participant. In that distinction lies much meaning. The environment that sustains the giant redwoods is complex and worthy, but it stands as something outside of human experience. A week in canoe country, on the other hand, is an intimate immersion in a natural setting where human interaction with the environment is required. One can hardly think of north woods canoe country without including people in the picture. People paddle the lakes, carry the portages, fish the waters, hike onto the ridges, and make camp on the prominences. The tradition is one of human activity, human involvement, human re-creation. A visit to the Boundary Waters erases the boundary that separates men and nature. More is required of a wilderness traveler, but more is received, too, and there is the superlative addition of the sense of active involvement. A place like Muir Woods is a park, set aside. Canoe country is a way of life, in which the traveler becomes an environmental agent or participant.

Broken Paddles

My outfitter-guide business is quite a small one, and so at times I try to save money by ordering some of my supplies with other outfitters. One of my needs is for paddles, but over time it has become harder and harder to be able to order paddles with the other outfitters. One after the other, they have arrived at the same conclusion: When I call around to ask who's ordering paddles, I hear, "We're getting those aluminum ones this year. They cost more, but they put an end to broken paddles. That's the way to go. No maintenance and a good guarantee. Why don't you switch over to the aluminum ones with us?"

Well, I've had my hands on a few aluminum paddles. They surely are "indestructible," and they have all the charm of an aluminum broom handle. They feel dead in the hands, they have no spring the way wood does, and their grip area often promotes holding the paddle with the lower hand well above the throat—a habit I try to get people to break. So, there are many reasons why I don't buy aluminum paddles, even if they are in some respects superior.

On one of my excursions to round up paddles I was at an outfitter's place and was going through his "old" stock of wooden paddles. I was selecting out the lightweight ones, because a light paddle takes less effort to swing, something you appreciate when you're paddling all day. One of the people who worked there made a special point of criticizing my selection of light paddles, because the light ones would be of less dense and therefore weaker wood. Of course that's true as far as it goes. But I wasn't there to select strong paddles so much as I was there to find good paddles for paddling. There's a difference, and in my line of work I teach people how to use a paddle so that they don't have to handle it as if it were a bludgeon for beating the water. Anyway, I explained I had a reason for wanting light paddles and went on with my selecting.

When I was done I had two dozen used, light, palm-gripped, wooden paddles that had already been "field tested." As I went to pay for them the outfitter said, "Well, I won't be missing those old things, though I have to keep a few wooden paddles for the old-fashioned folks or for the occasional nut who's on a purist or nostalgia trip. Really, Harry, you ought to switch over to the nonbreakable paddles. They'll save you so much work and you won't even have to worry how people might abuse your paddles."

What he said explained *everything* for me. Even though I could have taken some umbrage at being lumped in with the purists and nuts, his comment paid me a considerable compliment. He said he didn't have to bother about *how* people used his paddles. For me as a guide, the *how* of paddling is my bread and butter. Far from being a bother, I find teaching and working with people on their paddling to be a reward in itself. It is enjoyable, and my competitor was missing out on that part of the joy of being in outfitting. For him, the issue was clearly economic. Paddles that can't break are cheaper in the long run, and they don't require that you do anything more with them, including instructing people on how to use them. In my case, a paddle is a tool for reaching people and getting them to interact with wild country and deepen their understanding of wilderness travel. They are going to spend many hours each day with paddle in hand, and I want them to develop a feel and appreciation for what's going on between their hands and the water, via the paddle. If I can use a paddle that *might* break as a vehicle for teaching better than I can use a foolproof paddle, then I'll take the more delicate paddle every time. My clients are worth that little bit of extra effort, because I've found the one thing that's better than the foolproof paddle, and that's the paddler who's not treated as a fool.

Guiding Across the Ocean

Is there a fraternity that includes all guides? I think not. For example, many guides work in a production routine and are expected to help a client land his limit in fish or a trophy animal. That sort of guide inhabits a work world that is alien to me, as an outdoor-instructional guide. In my encounters with hunting or fishing guides, I've become quite aware of the pressures they work under, and I found little to share with them in terms of attitude. But I have had one memorable encounter with a trek guide from the Republic of South Africa. His job was to lead week-long foot journeys to observe wildlife in wilderness preserves.

Your reaction is probably much the same as mine was: I couldn't have found a guide whose experience would be more far removed from mine. Canoe country wilderness has precious little in common with the plains and scrub of Africa. On a physical level we had vastly different problems to deal with in our camping and daily travel. I found his tale of red, fist-sized (but harmless) spiders that would rush out of the darkness toward the campfire to catch moths pretty horrifying, while he found the thought of my hordes of barely visible biting flies to be intolerble. And there was, of course, the obvious contrast about available water. He had to share bathing and cooking water with the wildlife, which relied on "holes" dug in the beds of rivers that only occasionally had surface water.

My African friend told of an experience he'd had on one of his more unusual trips, a day-long canoe excursion along a coastal estuary. In that adventure one of his canoes had been bitten completely in half by a startled hippo, leaving (luckily) both paddlers unharmed in the severed bow and stern sections. Nothing could measure my relief at never having had to contend with hippos in the Boundary Waters.

Such wildlife was too hazardous for my tastes, but the African guide was here to learn of a danger I took quite for granted and seldom bothered to

124

consider with the sort of fear his wildlife story had given me. He could take a hippo in stride and acknowledge it as an acceptable risk. What struck him with fear was cold, which killed more unprepared South African trekkers venturing into the mountains than the wildlife did. He had come to the States to gain experience and training in dealing with cold conditions.

During his stay we talked at length about cold temperatures, hypothermia, and special clothing. The informational part of his visit having gone well, we began to drift toward other topics; he talked about the Zulu people and I told him something about Native Americans. In time we were relaxed enough to begin to "read" one another. I could tell where one of his remarks was going, because my style of camping was wilderness-style, like his, and we both kept things simple. When I would explain some fine point of portaging, he'd catch on to my "economy of effort" approach and smile in recognition of that philosophy. We recognized common areas, and our talks took a more intuitive turn as each of us discovered familiar content in the otherwise strange terrain of our respective guiding stories.

I remain impressed by how consistently wilderness-style guiding works. I found that he and I had the same goal for our clients — to create an environment where they can begin to experience wild country on a personal level. His treks required hours-long, single file, silent walks through scrub country where wildlife could be seen, studied, and enjoyed. My trips required hours of steady paddling and concentration to maintain course in order to traverse lakes where we'd enjoy new outdoors environments and further camping.

In both cases much repetitious physical activity becomes liberating. It allows the mind to explore the surrounding environment while simultaneously reassessing past, urbanized experiences.

The African guide and I also discovered that we preferred to keep ourselves in the background, trying to establish leadership that was more functional than flashy. He on foot, me seated in the stern of a canoe; we had both found a simple, humane teaching situation that cherished both environment and society. In wilderness-style living we had both encountered the freedom gained by limiting material possessions.

Yes, it was a good and rewarding experience for me to spend a few weeks with a guide from across the ocean. I could grow quite philosophic and posit a fascinating number of interesting observations, but I'll confess that much of what I *really* recall is absurdly (enough to make me cherish it all the more) human.

I remember the lively, personal tales of guiding and of living in the bush. I came to recognize the quiet role of the guide's elderly Zulu friend who brought up the rear of the marching column, carrying his spear. I could appreciate the humorous incidents at water holes, and I could feel the consternation of people who wished to take a quick bath (when surface water was present), only to be put off by the surroundings, which gave miles and miles of visibility, almost like removing your clothes in the middle of a huge stage.

There was one story, however, that was a bit better than the rest. It was a tale about a guide my friend worked with, a man in his thirties. This other guide was charged with the responsibility of supervising a walking tour for a dozen teenaged girls, accompanied by a matron as their chaperon. The word "matron," itself, implies a different social order than the one most Americans are familiar with, but the story continues with the guide leading this group, all very proper.

Early one morning just after dawn, the guide's sensitive ear detected noise, and he awoke just as a black rhino (very dangerous and temperamental) stepped into the clearing, moving slowly toward the line of sleeping girls, where the matron rested, too. Knowing he had to act quickly, the guide leaped up (unfortunately not having time to don his shorts) and loudly yelled the first things that came to mind.

His curses did not deter the rhino, but they did wake some of the girls, who looked in astonishment at this naked man swearing at the top of his lungs. And because they were looking at him, they did not see what he was yelling at, the rhino was getting ever closer.

Still cursing, he grabbed a nearby piece of firewood and threw it toward the rhino, but it missed, fell short, and nearly brained the matron. The guide then grabbed his rifle and fired two rounds toward the beast, which finally turned and went back into the bush at a trot.

The two shots, of course, roused every girl in the group, and the first thing their wide eyes beheld was the guide standing naked with his rifle. Quite shaken, he continued to say lowly things about the parentage and sex habits of rhinos as he slipped on some pants and then sat down on his pack, fetched out a bottle, and took a good slug to calm himself. All the while the girls were getting louder and louder as they compared facts, some having seen the rhino, most not, and all quite shaken by the episode. The guide, while rather embarrassed, reasoned that he had, after all, saved the girls from being trampled, and considered the incident to be over and done with, best forgotten.

Nonetheless, after the group was delivered safely home, the attending matron wrote a strong letter of protest, accusing the guide of consuming alcohol, using foul language, and "exposing" himself in front of the girls. She apparently didn't believe there had been a rhino at all, and assumed that the guide had simply said there was an invading animal as an excuse for his exhibitionistic splurge.

In explaining the matter to his superiors, the guide remained calm and factual. He pointed out that the matron had been sleeping at the end of the line and would have been the first person trampled had the rhino not been turned aside. The guide explained that whether she realized it or not, the matron was alive to complain because he'd fired his gun before putting on his pants and not after. Considering her letter of protest, however, he'd begun to think that perhaps he should have taken the time to slip on his briefs, allowing the rhino to convince her of its presence.

Nature's Voice

Some of nature's calls have a special place in the heart, like the loon-song or white throated sparrows calling ("Oh Sweet Canada, Canada, Canada!") in thick balsams or alder. Those sounds remind me of many wild settings. Other sounds, like the crackle of blackbirds on cattails and swamp reeds, bring to mind a more limited type of wild setting, the kind of place I'd only be passing through.

I am amazed to find I've made such discriminations and categorizations. I'd not intended it. But I know the sound of a distant frog entering the water, of mouse-rustled leaves outside the tent late at night, of passing night ripples on an otherwise calm lake. Each noise has its own meaning, its own season and intent.

Recall the way a drying leaf sounds as it strikes a bare, dead branch during a strong and fitful wind. The sound expresses part of nature's cycle, as surely as does the sound of breezes in red pines or the predawn buzz of mosquito hordes. Hearing a fish jump, can't you guess its size, species, even the food it was after? There's a bundle of neighborhood news in the sounds that help construct and define our immediate environment.

Take, for example, the sharp hiss of wind clawing through stiff tiger tail reeds along shore. That voice of nature says something distinct from the grassy reeds that bend with the wind in snake dance surface patterns, acres of muted stems, the most subtle of strings.

Having been forced, of late, to spend less time in the bush, I'm discovering how a single sound can represent so much. Water lapping against a log is distinct from the sound that radiating ripples breaking round a rock make protruding through the evening calm. Each of those sounds is a familiar pattern bringing back, in a rush, a total picture. A sound reminds me of places, people. A paddle gurgles, slow paddling. "Whip-whizz" goes a fishing pole, monafilament darting, lure plopping by the lily pads, then "click," the retrieve starts its smooth purr, every few seconds, a drop of water falling from the lead eyelet. In those sounds, a complete picture. I am happy. I'm paddling while someone I care for fishes. The sounds do not express my inner joy, yet, somehow the two are linked.

I find myself listening more intently these days. In nature's voice I'm reminded of so many times and places. I was busy living them as they occurred, and I'm quite sure I didn't convey the fuller side of my feelings to those around me. Indeed, I probably was unaware of how much I loved what I was doing or of how much my companions meant to me. I sensed, I suppose, how important they were, but some insecurity or fear kept me silent, acting with reserve.

Raindrops on canvas, the sound of a canoe rocking on small waves, the "clunk" of firewood dropped on earth's drum in the morning—the sounds of my familiar past. Unseen rapids in a gorge near a portage, the buzz of a hovering dragonfly, a strong gust musses the tops of the aspens, which applaud in a burst of green leaf claps—the sounds of nature's domain, uninfluenced by my individual efforts. Sound *is* time passing, shifting away, gone, but for an echo.

"Chic-a-dee-dee-dee, chic-a-dee-dee-dee," I hear two birds in a black spruce, singing against the wind. A few feet away, you are gathering dead-dry spruce twigs, collecting a mass, snapping them off in a compact bundle. The birds fluff themselves, wind stirring their feathers, as you turn toward me. You are smiling, cheeks red, your breath visible; something from inside yourself glimpsed and then gone. The loud "ping" of a large raindrop announces the coming rain by banging the cook-kit fry pan. The alarm sounded is then repeated as the first big drops whack thimbleberry leaves before establishing a steady pattern on the rain tarp. Our shelter, rain-tight, sends a stream of water off the low corner. The fire, not hot enough yet, but protected by our shelter, burns with a wet hiss and occasional dull pops. It grows slowly to a hot burning fire with a bed of embers, one of which will tumble too far from the glowing pile, crackle in slow death, grow black, inner fire extinguished.

The chill of night comes, with trees dripping onto cold bare earth and sodden leaves. The fire burns with more determination, hot enough to smack its lips around fresh pieces of wood, eager tongues consuming branches and split pieces, maintaining our defensive circle of light and heat against a nasty-dispositioned night. The fire is a steady hunger, no words from its blastfurnace mouth, only the sound of burning in harmony with night breezes moving night-shrouded branches.

We talked, I am sure, as we had on other nights, of minor things, passing chuckles, of the cold, our hands busy staying warm as we toasted them near the fire or cradled our cups. I'd no reason to think the pattern would end, no reason to believe there was any urgency to say those small things so often lost in the crush of days.

The years since then have left an accumulation of desire. A familiar sound projects scenes of visited places, reminding me of what was and wasn't left complete. Hungry desire urges one to go back and do it all, as if one ever could. Desire's hunger, though, drove me in earlier years to regret not having said more to you. Unable to go back in fact, my mind went back to attempt reliving, such ruminations ending in regret. Yes, I was sad about teasing you over your wobbly humor. I wished I'd been more accepting and good-humored about that. But I've had to set aside the sadder notes. What I didn't say is matched in measure by what you did not say. For both of us, another voice spoke constantly at our side, everything from whispers to dramatic storms. What I neglected was spoken for me in nature's code— "chic-a-dee-dee-dee, chic-a-dee-dee-dee."

Wind Words

Wind from the West,
black clouds building
into purple-edged boils,
where lightning flashes,
too distant to be heard
above the steady
leaf-rattling blow
growing stronger, flattening the waves
while making them dance,
like sharp, harmonic points.
The West wind is storm wind.
Before the big drops spatter
a drummed warning on tent roofs,
violently shaking the trees,
the camper hastily rechecks
his gear. He hopes
for the best, never knowing
where the storm's hand
will fall most heavily.

North wind comes at the tag end
of a late summer storm.
A gray, rainy day turns sharp.
The first flakes of the season
are wind-fired to earth,
quickly melting.
They are omens from a wind
born where the tundra freezes
for another season, from where the geese
fled, where polar airs and polar bears
are the predatory image. Huge,
lonely spaces give the wind
an extra chill, a shiver of awe.
This long-distance traveler
will howl through the forest
through months of tree-groaning cold.

Sunrise wind, coming from the Atlantic,
following the course of the Great Lakes
into the interior. The East wind's
like sunrise—gentle, imperceptible,
then steady. In spring, this first
warming wind carries hints of
fresh leaves, newly exposed ground,
early blossoms, as nature (denied for months)
responds to sunrising breezes with
a riot of pungent, earth smells.

The South wind comes to us
from across the Great Lake, Superior.
Warm southern air collides
with Superior's cold zone,
then travels on as fog,
misty wisps of prairie smells
and farm country heat, (palpable)
becoming North's airborne version
of hotter climes. A hint
of the hot, humid plains remains,
but the new version's more temperate.
The heat moves north
in rolling waves of South wind,
pouring north like breakers
bound for a distant shore,
carrying the flow of languid summers
across a cold inland sea.

But when these winds
have passed me by,
these seasons run due courses,
these impressions added to
so many more, enough
to make the timing right,
I'll be ready for
the last wind, hoping
with my final breath,
to catch the breeze
and know its meaning
as I journey on.
These winds, the ones concerning
you and I today, will not matter,
but for a few details.

The details, then, are symbols
for what's already occurred, but
nonetheless, I ask that what remains
be carried north, my truest direction.
I wish my Anishanabe friends, the ones
I'd always wanted to know better,
to bury me as one of them.
In their tongue, let them say
the words I don't know,
but have always understood.
Let there be no marker
on my spirit house
of boards or bark,
There will be an entrance
for the wind to enter,
perhaps bearing a fragment
of my spirit in passing,
another wind-borne element
recognizing another cycle
in the cycling Hoop of Life.
Season after season, the wind
enters and leaves my djibe'gûmig,
which slowly decays
to a soft, rounded hummock,
where on the most quiet of summer days
the wind will find
a place to playfully wave and rustle
the sweet, bending grass.

"Góralu, Czy Ci Nie Zal"

I remember my grandfather playing his fiddle, off key, the notes slurred. His singing was of a similar quality, crude, plaintive, coming from some deep, personal drive. His music took him back to Poland, and, I suppose, to the days of his youth. The old man would walk through the house, back and forth, fiddling and singing for all he was worth, lost in his own world, grandchildren like wind-blown leaves following before and after, and all the while my grandmother and the other mothers trying to set bowls of golden chicken soup or heaped plates of food on the table. With the house full of people and chaos, grandfather never sat down to eat but just kept strolling and playing, stopping in the kitchen for another slug of beer, and so inspired, continuing with another song.

It was his wish that I learn the violin; I was the eldest grandson, so the tradition passed on to me. I did learn "Flow Gently Sweet Afton," and that's as far as I got. It bothered me that I didn't have the enthusiasm to learn the violin, because it seemed as if I was letting the old man down. He, after all, had bought a used violin, taken it completely apart, rebuilt it *his* way, and then presented it to me as both gift and legacy. Before his death he'd begun to make complete instruments from scratch using tools, jigs, and presses he designed and built. He wanted to make violins with souls, but it was not for me to inherit his gift.

To this day I can play no musical instrument. Instead, I remember what came from the old man's heart. Most of the grandchildren were afraid of him, and I was, too, but I was able to glimpse just a bit of the side he kept covered with harsh words. He could be ornery, but because of his music I'd seen what his heart knew.

I remember how often he told me that I'd better turn out to be good for something. As a machinist and tool and die maker, he knew what he was good for, and he made no bones about being fearful that I'd be useless if I didn't watch myself and buckle down. He took huge pride in bringing out handcrafted item after skillfully constructed item, each showing his skill and mastery of metals and machines. His nickname was Stainless Steel Joe, because he liked to work in that material, and as proof he remade a Volkswagen, substituting stainless steel for the body parts and core of the car. He was very sincere and dedicated about his work, and you could feel his intense interest and enthusiasm regarding the problems and challenges of his trade.

Aside from prodding me to make something of myself, my grandfather wanted me to know what it was to be a Góral. A Góral is a Pole, but a special sort of Pole. A Góral is from the Tatry mountain area, and to him everyone else is a flatland farmer. Górals were mountaineers and not fond of being governed or controlled. They led trade expeditions down the challenging river gorges below the mountains. They felt themselves to be independent and free. Their language was not the refined, Latinized Polish of Warsaw; they spoke the hillbilly Polish of the mountains, low in class but large in freedom.

When grampa would sing a Góral song there was a different quality in his voice and in his playing. It was as if he were a seasoned Gypsy performer playing for himself outside his wagon. And, when he started "Góralu, Czy Ci Nic Zal," the whole family would stop, all those who could speak Polish joining in, feeling the song, sometimes even shedding a tear or two because of the music's message.

"Góralu, Czy Ci Nie Zal" is actually part of a question, and the song itself has many verses. The following is a short version of the spirit of that song, starting with the question, 'Góralu Czy Ci Nie Zal?"

> *Góral, do you not remember?*
> *The hills of your youth, of home?*
> *Góral, no matter where you may wander,*
> *Your heart always wanders these hills.*

I never lived up to what my grandfather had in mind, but I turned out rather true to form, for a Góral. My grandfather left Poland to escape the confines of rural life, and he fully embraced the offerings of the industrial, machine age. But here am I in the New World doing exactly the sort of thing my Góral ancestors did for centuries in the Polish mountains and on the raging rivers. The irony of that isn't lost on me, nor are some of the other, unusual connections.

For example, I live near the Grand Portage Indian Reserve where the local Ojibway people do excellent, elaborate floral decorations and include the use of the money cowrie shell (which they call the Megis) in both decorations and legend. Just exactly how a nearly tropical seashell comes to be part of the tradition of people located far inland in the north is one of those mysteries I can't explain. Nor can I explain what I saw in Poland while going down a river in the foothills of the Tatry mountains. Our guide was a Góral who wore the local costume: trousers with an intricate, embroidered design, a vest with a colorful, elaborate floral decoration, and on his head a flatish hat with a rim decorated with money cowrie shells.

Henry David Thoreau (his mother called him David Henry) referred to Native Americans as the original poets, the namers of things. I found a similar quality in the Górals of the mountains, who named an isolated, crag-enclosed lake, Morskie Oko, the Eye of the Ocean. The name was both poetic and deeply rooted in a love of natural things.

I have no delusion that only Native Americans or Górals have close attachments to the natural world. Intimate association with natural environments is part of the fabric of every human society and culture. We are creatures risen from Earth's gifts and nurtured in nature's academy. No matter what your background, a trip into a wilderness area where you can re-touch the natural world is really a trip back home. Returning home, you find your heart never left, no matter how long you've been away or how far removed.

Pole Shacks

I spotted an unnatural shape, which hung on a tree less than twenty yards off the portage path. I walked toward it, fairly sure it would turn out to be a coffee can lid tacked to a tree. Even before I reached it I could see other clues. What could have been mistaken for a fallen log turned out to be a rusted, moss-covered stovepipe. Poles, nailed and wired together, rotting boards, scraps of tarpaper, formed a sloping pile, the fallen-in roof and walls of a simple shack. A depression nearest the decaying shack was filled with cans and bottles cast off by the user—garbage remains long after the activity that generated it has stopped.

Looking around, I wondered what the purpose of this shack had been. Located at the end of a portage, and as simple as it was, it was probably used on a seasonal basis for fishing, hunting, or trapping. Perhaps twelve or fifteen feet long by eight feet wide when first built, the shack had hardly been spacious. This exceedingly simple structure would have protected one or two people from the elements, providing a rudimentary dry area that could be heated (the stovepipe was evidence that some form of stove had existed for heat and cooking). If the spot had been used for trapping or commercial net fishing, then the shack may have served to store items from season to season. But looking around, I couldn't tell for sure its exact age or function.

Over the years I've stumbled onto many such sites. Most of them are decayed away, like this one, disclosing only fragments. The shape of a board, even as it rots into the ground, is unnatural enough to be obvious, but bits of roofing, wire, nails, galvanized pails, broken dishes, glass, and the ever-present refuse pile are the most common fragments indicating prior use.

Those shacks near the ends of portages are the simplest. A few light poles were used to make a lean-to framework. Boards or split poles carried the tarpaper roofing, and more tarpaper covered the loosely constructed walls. One entered through a board door to an interior holding a pole bed, shelves, sheetmetal stove, and a few necessities. These shacks were much like wigwams, tarpaper rolls replacing the rolls of birch bark and reed used by native peoples (who constructed quite liveable homes this way). But pole shacks may have been kept crudely simple on purpose, because they weren't used often enough to require anything elaborate, and if visible or near portages, they would have been exposed to vandalism or unintended use.

In remote lands where recreational campers seldom go, or in out-of-the-way portions of well-traveled areas, one sometimes finds a more complete (even operational) shack. Quite by accident, I happened onto one while engaged in field assessment for the Archaeological Survey of Canada. Not visible from the lake, the shack sat in a damp, dark stand of reedlike spruce above a steep, bare granite dome. I was examining every outcrop along each lake, so I came upon this location, which had no boat landing area, giving a good clue as to which season it had been in use. More clues came from bits of snare wire and complete snares, stretcher frames, parts of broken trap springs. In vignette form, here was a glimpse into a trapper's subsistence pattern of life. Evidence of trapping and the lack of a boat landing confirmed that the shack was used only in winter, the season for prime fur. I may have been the last to see this particular structure, which was nearing collapse. Humble and frail as it was, in the depths of winter, such a prepared shelter, where you could light a fire and relax even a bit, would be both blessing and luxury.

Tucked away on a seldom traveled lake was another, more substantial, trapper shack. Made of logs rather than poles, the shack was built into a slope on an island. It looked almost like part of the hill. Only a rough board door, a small window, and a stovepipe identified this as a manmade structure.

Inside there was a low ceiling over a dirt floor on which sat a tiny cast-iron stove, much warped and broken. Behind the door hung old woolen pants and a jac shirt, spare clothes smelling of balsam pitch. Old boots hung upsidedown from a nail. This shack was very much still in use, and had its permit papers properly on display, as required in Ontario. You could be sure, too, that the trapper had nearby caches of material, food, and clothes to draw on; things that he wouldn't leave in the shack during tourist season.

I could imagine the scene in winter with the trapper inside after a day outdoors. No one around for many miles, mellow-gold light from the kerosene lantern would spill out the window onto a blue-cold, frozen landscape both frighteningly harsh and awesomely beautiful. If you could look inside on such a night, you'd see a few routine tasks being performed, such as eating, drying clothes, checking equipment. But you'd also be seeing the end of a way of life, flickering out of existence, growing as indistinct as the old, ripply-glassed window that allows your view, now obscured by frost.

That one-man trapper shack was more substantial than most pole shacks, and it was distinctly not the work of a Native American. Not so the fish camp I came across, hidden away on the shores of a narrow, weedy bay.

It was a Quonset-like structure, hardly six feet high at the center, with the door located on the end. When I pulled the door open, the interior seemed to come alive with scurrying red squirrels. As the fear-jolt passed, I stepped inside, where I had to walk slightly bent over. The frame of the shack was built of many limber poles, which formed an arch layered with more poles and a final covering of tarpaper and roofing. In all, this rambling, wigwam-like shack was thirty feet long by ten feet wide. The far end was filled with bunks and bed frames; the end, near the door, was a tangle of shelves, boxes, tables, and an impossible-looking cook stove. Another cook stove had been set up outside, as had wire frames for spreading opened fish prior to smoking them. The frames stood man-high. I recalled seeing one end of a smoky, creosoted piece of canvas sticking out of a box in the shack, and I assumed that it had been used to cover the frames and hold in the smoke. From what I could tell, this was at one time a native-style seasonal fish camp used by a cooperating group of people. Probably the camp was used for fall net fishing. The catch went directly toward family subsistence and any surplus was sold to provide some cash.

Not far from that location was one of the snuggest, most complete shacks I've ever come across. It was built of logs and had a board floor and roof. Inside there was the odor of cold wood smoke, oakum from chinking logs, and kerosene. The almost sour smell of the closed, vacant cabin reminded me of places my family used on our vacations north when I was growing up.

As a boy, I stayed in some quite unpretentious shacks located near the spots where we spent our days fishing for walleye. These places had character (often too much so for the women of the party). The best of the lot is still in use. When I was seven, the path from lake to cabin was a steep, up-hill struggle. When last I visited the site, I walked the incline without breathing hard, and I wondered about the small boy who had labored his way up the rise. Inside the cabin that long-ago summer, my mother had waged a continual battle against dirt, every new mouse dropping a cause for much scrubbing, especially of eating utensils. I think she and my aunt spent that entire vacation sterilizing things. Even so, the cabin/shacks used by tourists were well above the level of tarpapered pole shacks used by people scratching a subsistence living from the area.

The sagging hulk of a fairly substantial board shack sits near the entrance from a large lake into an extensive interior bog. Another is a decayed mound on a riverbank campsite located in an area with numerous moose. One was built on a point where its occupant, probably a trapper, cleared a large garden, meaning he used this location in summer, too. I know of another spot that has its typical pole shack, but has, as well, a cluster of minishacks for storage. That collection is built on ground far too wet for summer use, except by someone wearing waders. A larger, log shack with two bunks was built above a rapids. Hidden from view, the shack had a large refuse pile, suggesting many years of use. A local told me about a place where he'd "camped" with his dogs twenty-five years earlier, and sure enough, you can still see the area he cleared off when he worked his trap line. I can recall dozens of locations that once held shacks, the majority of which are rubble.

Most shacks suffer from the same basic defects. They are built for temporary or seasonal shelter, and they are most often the work of lone individuals, therefore the emphasis is on economy of material and effort. Low-pitched roofs are easy to build, so most shacks are built that way. The builder simply sets numerous support poles under the roof to carry the snow load when he's not there. If the shack is visible, tourists who use it inevitably remove the supports and use them for summer fires. The following winter, the roof will fall in if there's enough snow. In some cases, too, the original user just abandons the shack when it's no longer needed. The simplest shelters have nothing worth going back for, so they are written off. Without a yearly "fix" of tarpaper, these shacks quickly grow leaky, and the moisture speeds up rotting and weakening—they soon collapse. Many of these shacks were built as little more than semi-permanent tents, never intended to endure.

But some abandoned locations offer surprises and present enigmas. On a large Canadian lake with many delicate points and hundreds of large and small islands, I got lost while looking for a seldom-used portage I'd been told about. Coasting along the shore searching for it, I approached a tiny sand beach with a man-tall granite rock standing guard like a sentinel. A much larger, breadloaf rock formed an unusual island just offshore. The location was striking, inviting. That's when I noticed the butt end of a weathered board protruding at the high water or berm line. Looking more carefully, I saw what could only be a trail, hidden by the guard rock. Behind it was the hint of a clearing, just visible with the approach of fall and the end of the growing season.

My companions and I beached our canoe and soon found that the guard rock did indeed mask the start of a trail. A few feet up, we came upon the wreck of a cedar-strip boat. It was almost flattened through rot and snow weight from past seasons. In this condition it presented the ideal location for ants, which rushed with alarm as my boot tapped on the hull. I noted that the bottom of the boat had been covered in galvanized sheet, indicating it had been used to the fullest extent of the season, metal sheeting being ice protection. The ruin of another, simpler boat lay nearby, its wide-board sides still standing above a flat bottom now sprouting grass.

The path led to a clearing several hundred feet wide (big, for bush country), and filled with waist-high grass just beginning to turn toast-tan. A line of trees had been left between lake and clearing, making the location hard to spot. I soon discovered why the site seemed to be arranged for privacy: The clearing held a surprising collection of small buildings.

A low log building with a door you had to duck by nearly a foot held only a double bed, with room for little else. The door lay leaning on one hinge, barring further entrance to the interior, where most of the rear portion of the roof had fallen in on the bed. Short roof spans usually last the longest unattended, so something had certainly caused this miniscule sleeping cabin to cave in.

Farther along, a larger cabin held several beds and a rusted stove, tipped and useless. The roof obviously leaked, giving the place a moldy smell, but with some work the roof on this one could be saved. Of course, campers don't carry materials for repairing buildings, so someone would have to make a special effort to come back. It didn't seem like that was going to happen, and this cabin was nearing the critical point where it would quickly become completely useless, wasted.

Another building, the only one constructed with boards, was built like a pantry filled with shelves, the floor now littered with rusty tins and broken glass. A few yards away, set on the edge of the clearing against a green backdrop of balsams, was a "fancy" four-hole outhouse, a sure sign that numbers of people had used this location at the same time.

In the center of the clearing, though, sat the main cabin, built of large pine logs weathered gray with time. The door, intact, unlocked, opened onto a Spartan but complete interior. Smelling of oakum and dust, the first room was for sitting; chairs and benches and tables provided seating for at least ten. The next room, with a curtain door, was a bedroom with double bed, dresser, and clothes rod, which hung in the open.

The kitchen had been built lean-to fashion alongside the two main rooms. Here the cook stove, pots and pans, buckets, dishes, and silverware were all kept in order on shelves going from floor to ceiling. Though small, the kitchen seemed stocked to handle groups of people. Two skylights with screens had, no doubt, let out excess heat during cooking.

Going out, I stepped onto the porch, which was protected by a long, overhanging gable. Sun lit and warmed the porch. A grasshopper "click-click-clicked" in the obscuring grass. Behind me, one of my companions moved a chair, sending out the distinct vibrations of wood scraped across a board floor. As that sound went, I heard the wordless rise and fall of my two friends' voices as they talked quietly. From below, I heard waves coming into shore, driven by the same wind that sent land waves through the grass before me.

In that moment, like a blink, like a shudder passing through, I could sense the lives that had spent time here. And surely, at least one of those lives was drawn back here to keep the roof intact and the interior orderly. The feeling rippled through me, leaving my ears with a pulsing buzz, and I wondered whether, if I turned around at that moment, I would find my companions talking quietly or the spirits of those who had made this a temporary home?

Walking outside, I continued to sense a strange "timelessness" about the place, even as I tried to figure out how these cabins had been used. The space was far too small for a logging camp, but it could have been the family area for a camp boss, with the men's camp located elsewhere. If so, it seemed like an unusual sort of family home. If it had been a resort, it was awfully remote and offered odd accommodations. Possibly it was the work of a club, everyone cooperating on maintenance and use, the whole operation slowly falling to ruin as the task of upkeep fell on those who survived.

I found no answer for the mystery of that location, which still puzzles me. In time, like the simpler, low-roofed pole shacks it so closely copies, this camp will be neglected and slip into ruin. Low mounds of rotting logs, occasional glints of china or glass revealed where a bear has dug for ants in the infested, rotten logs, the camp will be gone, except for traces, except for memory, the hint of something elusive, which lingers where people once lived, and I hope, loved.

Crawl-in Cabin

A board-topped table,
worn oilcloth, edges frayed,
a glint of newness
where a corner's torn up.
Near the middle,
a circle wear-stain
marks the lantern's place
on the nighttime table.
Sun falling on the table, now,
sends a warm aroma
of oilcloth and kerosene,
no match for the meals
eaten here after hard days.
The wood box,
pungent with pine logs,
contains one with a visitor,
a boring beetle,
snug in his home.
"Crunch"—then a long pause,
"Crunch"—he'll keep on
until his home
becomes his crematorium,
the smell of woodsmoke
scenting the morning bacon,
warming the chill of night.
By the door,
a can for outboard,
mixed-gas, oily and fragrant.
Spilled in the boat,
it will be slippery,

coating the boat bottom,
permeating your boots.
Cast-off furniture,
things that won't be missed
if the place burns
or uninvited guests get rowdy,
the interior is a mix
of lives and style—
a homemade table,
a once elegant smoking stand.
Here and there
a crack of light
slips through the wall
at some gap in a board,
or where the creosote-smelling oakum
has slipped loose.
The cast-iron stove top
makes a distinctive sound
once heard, never forgotten.
The floor is a history
of wear and weather
carried in on tired feet.
Hard times
and good times
lived here
on the same slender reed,
sharing a stalk
of hope.
How familiar, reassuring,
the sound of water bucket and dipper,
Left afloat,
the dipper
slowly sinks,
hitting the bottom
with a satisfied, galvanized clunk.
The humble intimacy
of life lived and worked
on such terms
is never lost.
The day-to-day press of effort
almost drags the life
out of a person,
leaving you
so weary, weary of work.

In some seasons,
only two activities—
labor and sleep.
Yet, when work is done
or nature's called a halt,
you're suddenly bored senseless,
reading the same magazine
over and again.
Restlessness will give way
to sleep,
needed for renewal
after full days,
which mask what's missing.
The dreams of those dog-tired
are not fanciful dips
or trips of delight,
the dreamer's a survivor
fighting upward,
a long, struggling swim.
Surfacing at wakefulness,
groggy, sore, feeling beat,
you force-drag yourself up,
to stand, urinating,
outside the door
feeling the chill.
Going in,
returning to bed
is a tempting thought,
but a fire in the stove
wins out,
because you want to be warm,
because there are so many things
to do.
Heating up,
the fry pan smokes.
Its surface wiped clean,
never washed,
it's oily-seasoned,
just as you were instructed
to keep it.
Boiled coffee
in a finger-burning cup
washes down the meal.

Tidy up,
leave things in order,
get the day's activity started,
but before you step outside,
a recurring, passing thought,
something oft noted:
No matter how you clean,
there's a pervasive odor,
sour, like vinegar or pickles,
which seems to come from the pores
of the place.
If poverty has a smell,
that is its odor.
But such poverty
comes replete
with new days, which,
no matter how impossible or tiring,
burst with sight and sound,
detailed and complete.
Feasts,
universes of sensation
carried back to the cabin each night.

The Guide's Final Word

To those I've paddled with and to my readers . . .

If ever I've done, said, or written something which has made an impression on you, I hasten to remind you that I am not the cause of any good effect. If you have found something of value, it is not because of me. I have been, at most, only a guide, or sometimes the archaeologist scratching at the surface. If I have uncovered anything of worth, dear companions, please know that I have only made you more aware of what was waiting to be uncovered in your own spirit. If I have ever written words you found to be "true" remember, please, that I am only pointing out to you such truth as was already written in your heart.